BIONIC

e

TEAM
WORK

BIONIC

e

TEAM
WORK

How to Build Collaborative
Virtual Teams at HyperSpeed

Jaclyn Kostner, Ph.D.

Dearborn™
Trade Publishing
A **Kaplan Professional** Company

This publication is designed to provide accurate and authoritative information in regard to the subject matter covered. It is sold with the understanding that the publisher is not engaged in rendering legal, accounting, or other professional service. If legal advice or other expert assistance is required, the services of a competent professional should be sought.

Vice President and Publisher: Cynthia A. Zigmund
Editorial Director: Donald J. Hull
Senior Acquisitions Editor: Jean Iversen
Senior Project Editor: Trey Thoelcke
Interior Design: Lucy Jenkins
Cover Design: design literate inc.
Typesetting: Elizabeth Pitts

Printed in the United States of America

01 02 03 10 9 8 7 6 5 4 3 2 1

Library of Congress Cataloging-in-Publication Data

Kostner, Jaclyn.
   Bionic eteamwork : how to build collaborative virtual teams at hyperspeed / Jaclyn Kostner.
     p. cm.
   ISBN 0-7931-4834-0
   1. Virtual work teams — Management — Handbooks, manuals, etc. 2. Business communication — Handbooks, manuals, etc. I. Title.
   HD66 .K678 2001
   658.4′02′0285 — dc21   2001002055

Dedication

To Jim—
my life partner, soulmate, and mentor

CONTENTS

I am grateful for the host of wonderful people that helped me bring this very important message to the world. Words can't express how delightful it has been to meet you, learn from you, and now hopefully give something important back to each of you.

The phenomenal name for this book—*Bionic eTeamwork*—was crafted by Jim Kutsko. His creative mind enabled me to articulate a new generation of teamwork. *Bionic eTeamwork* gives people the right words to represent a new world of teamwork. Thank you, Jim, for helping me shape this book into one that provides value and inspiration for business people around the world.

On another level, a very warm thank you goes to my core virtual team. To Judith Briles, my friend and mentor, who helped me find the right agent. To Robert Vicek, who suggested the *e* in the title *Bionic eTeamwork.* To Robert and Lisa Vicek, Paula Noonan, and Pat and Alan Whitelock—each for reading, proofing, and giving me fantastic feedback. I couldn't have done it without all of you.

I am especially grateful for the inspirational leaders and teams whose stories give all of us so much hope. Thank you for sharing your wisdom, insight, and best practices. To Jimmy Treybig of Tandem Computers, Howard Sorgen of Merrill Lynch, Neal Martini of Hewlett Packard, Anthony Robbins of Silicon Graphics, Dr. Eric Schmidt of Novell, Maridan Clements of Philips, Wendy Johnson of Chute Gerdeman, Tom Ruddy of Xerox, Robert Vicek of Lockheed-Martin, Ann Balaban of Texas Instruments, Steve Cook of Northrop Grumman, Marilyn Stangle of Lucent, Heather Dixon of Intel, Greg Dickson of Dow, Russell Kern of Kern Direct Marketing, Keith Glennan of Logicon, Jerry Pederson of Compaq Computers, Chuck Roberts of IBM, Kent Harmon at Texas Instruments, Laura Schmidthammer at Alltel, and George Davis and Neil Deane of Davis and Deane.

Thank you also to the giants of this era whose quotes inspire us. To Bill Gates, Lou Gerstner, Dan Rather, Steve Ballmer, and Tom Brokaw.

Thank you to my agent, Doris Michaels. You are an inspiration! Thank you to my editor, Jean Iversen at Dearborn. It is a joy to work with you. It was fun getting acquainted online! I look forward to meeting you both face to face someday!

Thank you to the people that connected me to the leaders: Rob Casson, Kristy Ragones, Marsha Deminico, Selena Morris, Randy Lane, Eddie Miller, Ann Bacadin, Rebecca Michaels, Martha Reddington, Pat Pekary, Peggy Rayburn, Marlene Somsak, Jim Bowman, Bill Blane, Lisa Nyssonen, and Marika Kojo.

A special thank you to the companies whose collaborative technologies provide the foundation for *Bionic eTeamwork.* Your technologies are as critical to *Bionic eTeamwork* as e-mail and conference calls.

Last but not least, thank you to my photographer, Edward DeCroce. You are the only photographer in the world that takes pictures of me that I love. Thank you.

> *If the 1980s were about quality and the 1990s were about reengineering, then the 2000s will be about velocity.*
> **Bill Gates**
> *Business @ the Speed of Thought*

Fast is no longer fast enough. Incremental increases in speed just won't cut it in a new era that demands quantum leaps in virtual team performance. Velocity is about HyperSpeed—teamwork, performance, and results that are magnitudes faster than teams create today.

Does your team have what it takes to operate at Hyper-Speed? We live in a business world that operates in hyperdrive. Our virtual teams are surrounded by amazing speed-of-light technologies, but few virtual teams really operate at the speed of light. They accept technology, even achieve some advantages from it, but most are still waiting for the gigantic leaps in performance. By sheer will, and very long workdays, we are faster and more productive than we were five years ago. The adrenaline we're working on, however, can't last forever. Virtual teams have to get a lot smarter about how to increase their speed and supercharge their velocity.

Velocity demands that virtual teams are cohesive teams. In fact, they need to be more cohesive than ever, but with significantly less travel. Cohesiveness is about the team's humanity—its sense of team, level of trust, and degree of unity. Cohesiveness directly impacts the quality, frequency, and speed of collaboration that people will create *across* locations.

Up to this time, most virtual teams have relied heavily on travel to feel, create, or improve cohesiveness. Travel is like putting people in human mailing tubes. Although some travel is needed, it's too slow! Travel will keep your team from increasing velocity. Virtual teams have to get a lot smarter about how to create cohesiveness from afar—cohesiveness that is as high or higher than when people meet face to face. That moment is not in the future; it's here today!

A whole new generation of team has mastered how to dramatically increase their velocity and cohesiveness, from afar. They have broken through the wall and now act like beacons that take virtual teamwork to a record-breaking high—both in performance and in human relationships. They get the job done in a fraction of the time, while their team satisfaction and connectedness soar.

We become Bionic only when we master how we use our Bionic parts to supercharge human teamwork, speed team collaboration, increase trust from afar, improve morale across all locations, and produce phenomenally superior results.

In fact, these teams are so dramatically different than any kind of teamwork humans have created to date, that I have given this phenomenon a new name: *Bionic eTeamwork.*

Bionic is about using technology in ways that break through human limitations. Bionic is part human, part technology—but it is not about being robotic. Instead, it is about using technology in very creative ways to extend our human touch and human capability. All of us have Bionic parts: cell phones, pagers, laptops, e-mail, voice mail, and all of the other technologies that virtual teams use daily. Bionic parts, however, don't make us Bionic. We become Bionic only when we master how we use our Bionic parts to supercharge human teamwork, speed team collaboration, increase trust from afar, improve morale across all locations, and produce phenomenally superior results.

eTeamwork is about human collaboration, sense of team, and team results that people create from afar. eTeamwork isn't about sending a lot of e-mail to one another or talking frequently in conference calls. Instead, eTeamwork is team collaboration, interaction, and results (from afar) that are as good as, if not significantly *better* than, face to face. People that create eTeamwork know how to create a warm, spontaneous, high-energy environment from afar that satisfies and builds trust. People that create eTeamwork accept no compromise in the level of trust, sense of team, and real teamwork they can create, from afar. In fact, they often surprise themselves at how much fun it can be to work together in their digital space, compared to traveling to meet in a physical space.

Bionic eTeamwork is not hype. It is reality, and its results are breathtaking. At PartnerWorld 2001, Lou Gerstner, Chairman and CEO of IBM, gave a keynote address that focused on their 100,000 IBM Business Partners around the world. IBM embraces its business partners as full and critical members of the IBM team, not as contractors or vendors. In the speech, Gerstner hailed the IBM Business Partners for generating ⅓ of the company's $80+ billion in revenues. He also credited them for their major role in the rapid turnaround of IBM a few years earlier. That's Bionic eTeamwork at velocity!

Bionic eTeamwork requires teams to use more technology than they do now, including online collaboration technologies, such as web conference and electronic teamroom technology. (You'll learn more about how teams use these later in the book, or visit our Web site at <www.bionicteam.com>.) More importantly, it also requires new human best practices for each of those technologies. The key is for teams to use technology in ways that create a human environment for collaboration and trust that rivals anything any team has created to this point in history.

In this book, you'll see firsthand the best practices of some of the world's most creative leaders, teams, and individuals—those who have mastered how to create Bionic eTeamwork that blankets the globe. Here's a preview of these exciting pioneers.

- The CEO of SAS who transformed his dispersed organization's $20 million loss into a $55 million gain in one year, aligning people across Europe and the world at extraordinary levels.

- A team at Dow Chemical that rolled out a global process worldwide in ⅕ the normal time, with 100 percent consensus and buy-in—and no travel. The team bridged the interests of 132 sites, speaking 12 languages, and operating with 40 percent fewer people.

- The Hewlett-Packard/Canon team bridges two primary countries and cultures (Japan and the United States) as well as two separate companies. This alliance is recognized as one of the most successful partnerships (and ePartnerships) in the last century.

- A team of 24,000 at Xerox that circles the world, collaborating interactively via their Web site to deliver extraordinary service to their worldwide customer base.

- A team of 14,500 consultants at Merrill Lynch who use technology to create truly Trusted Global Advisors who serve their worldwide client base in an innovative, effective way.

- An 18-member team at Lockheed-Martin whose results saved the organization $5 million, made every decision with 100 percent consensus, accomplished results in ⅕ the normal time, and spent not one cent on travel.

- The CEO of Tandem Computer Company who built a $10 billion success story with a lean management structure, and an innovative communication strategy that inspired high performance teamwork throughout the company.

- A team at a major computer company that spans 28 offices, produces more revenues per person than any other division in the company, spends less money, and has the lowest turnover of any field organization in the company.

- A CEO of Davis and Deane, a worldwide consulting and training company, who creates close partnerships with contractors all over the world and delivers consistently excellent results. Together, they are a high-performance team in every respect.

- An Account Manager at Chute Gerdeman, who enhances client relationships with "virtual war rooms," saved 15 to 20 percent on their expenditures in each client engagement while increasing customer satisfaction.

- Teams from Boeing that use technology to shorten the project time by 90 percent, yet involve everyone in the process of setting the groundwork for success for the Boeing 777 aircraft.

- And many more from Lucent, Philips, Nortel, Novell, AT&T, and others.

As you can see, Bionic eTeamwork is a new breed of virtual team, streamlined to create exceptional performance across multiple locations. Bionic eTeams aren't enabled because they have technology. Rather, they are enabled because they know how to *use* technology to communicate and connect virtually. They operate at lightspeed, with high trust, because of the way they get connected while physically distant.

Teamwork isn't a technology. It doesn't happen because people plug in or log on to some online collaborative technology. It doesn't occur if people install software on the computer desktop. Teamwork is a human process, a human connection that creates magic. The differentiator is how virtual teams use their technology to facilitate that human process.

As business becomes more global, as we are surrounded by more technology, as we strive to be more productive with fewer resources—yesterday's model of effective virtual teamwork fails to make the team fast or cohesive enough. The only way to become fast enough is to learn how to create Bionic eTeamwork.

Whether your teamwork is between two members or among tens of thousands, the techniques these innovative Bionic eTeams used to inspire fast, cohesive teamwork apply to all sizes and types of virtual work groups. Bionic eTeamwork doesn't happen by chance. It happens by design. It's part of the plan. This book will help you create your plan for success in building collaborative virtual teamwork at Hyper-Speed.

Bionic eTeamwork doesn't eliminate the need for travel. It will, however, significantly reduce the need, because people will collaborate well without hopping on a plane or driving across town to be together.

Let me leave you with this thought. According to <www.biz traveler.org>, a site sponsored by the National Business Travel Association, the average business traveler will spend:

- 3 years in flight
- 2 years going to and from an airport
- 2.3 years waiting for a scheduled flight
- 0.9 years waiting for a connecting flight
- 0.25 years searching for a parking space

That's eight and one-half years!

Readers, we have a choice. Bionic eTeamwork gives you a whole new world of teamwork that you no longer have to travel to create. People don't have to be in one place to create energized, trusting, HyperSpeed teamwork.

Bionic eTeamwork—it's a much smarter way to increase velocity!

You will see some new terms that I coined for this book. Most of them begin with a small letter *e*. The *e* stands for electronic, as in e-mail. I use the prefix *e* to keep the focus on electronic communication—communication through technology, typically across vast distances.

So many of the words that people use now for virtual teams are too long. I wanted to simplify it. *Virtual team* is four syllables. *eTeam* is two. Simple! Short! Clear!

Here is a quick list of those words.

- **eTeam** A group of two to thousands that must work together and depend on each other, while communicating mostly through technology. (Sometimes the people are in the same building.)

- **eTeamwork** The fast, cohesive collaboration that people create by the way they communicate through technology with one another and/or work together, from afar.

- **eCommunity** An interactive, dynamic, synergistic connection that people create through technology.

- **eMeetings** Any kind of online or long-distance meeting, where people are not in one physical location; conference calls, video conferences, web conferences, group decision systems, and other groupware.

- **24/7** Around the clock, 24 hours a day, 7 days a week; independent of time or place.

- **eCollaboration** The level of interaction a group creates when they communicate through eMeetings, electronic teamrooms, or other collaborative technology.

- **InTouch** Trusting human connections and human relationships that Bionic eTeams intentionally build, linking people with each other and the joy of working together on a human level.

- **eMotion** A strong sense that the team is moving forward together with great speed, from afar; a strong human connection or sense of team that people create because of the way they collaborate through technology; preparation for rapid future movement as a team, from afar.

- **Moment of Truth** The human experience that results from behaviors that make a critical difference in success.

- **eWarmth** The ability to project an open, warm communication presence when communicating through technology.

- **eSurfdom** A critical contribution each member of an effective eCommunity makes to create a high-value site for all.

I am the author of this book, but I didn't write this book. I did not pick up a pen or key a single word on my keyboard. Nor did I hire anyone to take dictation or write it for me. I created this book differently than any of my other books. Based on this wonderful experience, I will do it again.

I didn't write this book. Using Dragon Naturally Speaking (speech recognition software), I *told* my story to my computer, just like I would tell it to a person. You see, I am Bionic. I am an ordinary human being, just like you. I am surrounded by a sea of technology, just like you. The factor that makes me Bionic, however, is that I use technology to extend my human touch—fast. I am passionate about building trust and teamwork when people do not share the same space. People have pain where they should have excitement. This book helps me touch your life with stories and insights that give you guidance. The technology lets me do it faster.

I write very early in the morning, usually starting at 2 or 3 AM, well before the sun comes up. I light a candle, put on some classical music, and open Microsoft Word and Dragon Naturally Speaking. I make a cappuccino, don a microphone, and start talking. While I watch the screen, I tell my story, just like I would in a keynote address, an executive briefing, or a conversation with a friend at Starbucks. As Dragon types my words on screen, it almost creates a sensation that the computer is listening. It keys my words exactly (unlike humans that want to change them or put their own words in place). Dragon even learned and understood some of the new words that I coined like eTeamwork, eCommunity, and eMotion—and typed them with the right capitalization!

Now, I haven't gone off the deep end. I have not given my computer a name. It's a machine. I do have a vibrant life away from my computer. Surprisingly, though, telling the story with Dragon was an amazingly personal way to write a book—Bionic style!

Bionic eTeams are a new generation of team worth being very excited about. They have broken through a huge barrier that makes working virtually significantly warmer, more productive, and more satisfying. This book is not about technology. It's about human connections and community that we create by the way people use technology.

We all have the power to warm our sterile virtual communication environment. As members of the human species, we have a compelling need to connect with one another. The exciting part is that we are no longer restricted by "place" to do that. I am grateful to the leaders who graciously shared their stories and their best practices. Their stories act as our mentors, guiding us in very specific ways to create sense of team, virtually.

I have posted a note on my computer that reads, "What did you do today to warm the eWorld around you?" It guides me throughout the day to build warmth, connections, and trust when I communicate virtually. After you read this book, make your list and stay focused on it. Together, we can make a difference!

We Have the Technology . . .

1

> The brief metaphor I am about to share has a great deal to do with you, your team, and all of the people you must collaborate with virtually every day.

The scene opens in a cold, sterile operating room. A severely injured man hovers between life and death as surgeons frantically rush to save his life. All of the people in the room move in a desperate frenzy to act quickly before time runs out. An accident has crushed both of the patient's legs, one of his arms, and one of his eyes—none could be saved. For the man on the table, the future looks grim. In the first phase of his metamorphosis, he faces a disability that will never go away. If he even survives, our fear is that the patient—Steve Austin—will be a mere shadow of his former self.

Then, in the background, we hear the voice of Oscar Goldman. He quietly, yet confidently, mutters a solution that is frightening but offers the only hope. "We have the technology," he says, and then pauses. With more energy and a faster pace, he continues, "We can make him *better* than he was before." His voice is now filled with assurance, an insight of technology that others don't yet see. He says with a tone that somehow combines a fact with a promise, ". . . faster, stronger, better."

In the next few seconds, we find out that Steve Austin did lose his legs, one arm, and one eye on that surgical table. Each is replaced with a bionic part, an artificial appendage with a strange new technology called a computer chip. Now he appears doomed to a life that seems more mechanical than human.

In this, the second phase of his technometamorphosis, we see a mechanized Steve Austin struggle to do the most basic human tasks, like walking. His movement is inconsistent. Sometimes, a step is a step forward. Other times, it's a fumble or an unexpected leap. The doctors and technicians refine and upgrade the technology, assuring Austin of its promise to make him better than he was before. At first, everything that Austin does seems slower and more challenging. With time and practice, he becomes more skilled in using his technology. He even begins to accept it into his life. Lacking the ease and swiftness of his human parts, though, Austin's life still appears to be forever compromised, forever diminished. We sense his pain as he struggles to find humanity through all the technology upon which he must depend for his very survival.

As the scene shifts again, months have passed. Clearly Steve Austin has survived. His life is, indeed, changed forever. Surprisingly, however, the changes are remarkably positive. In fact, they're extraordinary.

Why? Austin has completed his metamorphosis. He has arrived at the third stage of his technoevolution. Austin has transformed himself into the Bionic Man, primed with technology to do superhuman feats with ease and simplicity.

For example, on a good day, any of us would be happy to run at 6 miles per hour. With his Bionic legs, however, Steve Austin could run 60. In a single leap, ordinary humans can jump across a small puddle. In contrast, Austin could jump the length of a football field. His Bionic arm and his Bionic eyeball gave him even more superhuman capability. At last, he has reached the point in his journey where he is in touch with his humanity, yet is technocharged with immense power and speed. Fully Bionic, Austin once again feels happy, uniquely capable of making the community about him a better place.

The first phase of his metamorphosis was the Disabled Phase. Austin had technology forced on him, not by his choice. He resisted it and resented its intrusion on his humanity. Technology seemed such an inferior substitute that he mentally defied its forced entry in his life. The only way he felt human was without technology at all.

The second phase was the Mechanical Phase. Austin accepted technology and began to realize some of its potential. He learned how to get around, relying on his Bionic parts to do the things he used to do so easily and comfortably with his human parts. He often felt that technology constrained him, making his human movement feel robotic compared to before technology invaded. However, he hadn't taken his technology to the next level. He hadn't tapped into the immense power his Bionic parts offered.

The third phase was the Bionic Phase. Austin embraced his Bionic parts. *The technological part of his new self becomes an advantage that sets him apart from other human beings.* The technology is no longer just attached to him; rather, it is a part of him and makes him better. The Bionic Steve Austin realizes that first and foremost, he is a human being, not a machine. No matter how much technology is a part of him, he is driven not by a chip, a wire, or an electric circuit. Rather, he is driven by his heart, his soul, and his need to be connected with the human community around him. When he became Bionic, it didn't matter that he was part man, part machine. He was human first, foremost, and always.

Bionic eTeams are just like Steve Austin. They have Bionic parts: cell phones, pagers, e-mail, palm pilots, laptop computers, voice mail, web conference, and electronic teamroom tools. More importantly, they use their Bionic parts to create extraordinarily fast and cohesive teamwork, from afar. Bionic eTeams get their work done at HyperSpeed—in 30 to 90 percent less time—because of the way they embrace technology.

Bionic eTeams have evolved way beyond collaboration by e-mail and conference calls. Instead they create exceptionally fast and cohesive eTeamwork by the way they use all of their Bionic parts, especially their Web conference, electronic teamrooms, instant messages, and other team collaboration tools. (Throughout the book, you'll learn more about what these tools are and how teams used them to collaborate at HyperSpeed.)

When Bionic eTeams use any technology, no one is a passive participant. They travel less because their human collaboration when they connect via their Bionic parts is so effective. Bionic eTeams are masters in using these and all of their chosen team technologies in ways that dramatically speed team interaction, decision making, buy-in, collaboration, and results, from afar. These leaps in results are no accident, nor are they a natural evolution. They come out of a plan that makes people bond as a Bionic eTeam.

> Virtual teamwork depends on a lot of travel to keep team spirit, trust, and collaboration high. eTeamwork doesn't.

Bionic eTeams have also mastered how to create eTeamwork. eTeamwork is significantly more evolved than virtual teamwork. Virtual teamwork depends on a lot of travel to keep team spirit, trust, and collaboration high. eTeamwork doesn't. eTeams are masters at creating a sense of team, trust, and warmth by the way people interact through technology. eTeams are close-knit, high-collaboration, high-trust partner relationships that fluidly cross corporate boundaries, cultures, and languages to produce exceptional results in the marketplace. Bionic eTeamwork can be created in formal teams, informal teams, or with any distant individual that any of us have to work with to get our job done.

Bionic eTeams, of whatever configuration, are as happy, interactive, and connected in a digital space as virtual teams are in a physical space together.

In all three phases of Austin's evolution to the Bionic Man, he had the technology. The key factor that differentiated the three stages was how he used his Bionic parts. First he rejected technology, then he accepted it, and finally he embraced it in ways that gave him superhuman power. Teams that work in a virtual environment go through that same evolution.

This book will mention technology. Its real focus, however, is not on technology. It's at a much higher level: HUMANware™. Every team has SOFTware and HARDware. The differentiator is HUMANware: how people use technology to bond, build trust, collaborate, participate, and get results— with a significantly reduced need to travel.

The need for teams to evolve to Bionic eTeamwork isn't optional. It's a mandate for success.

We Have the Technology . . . But It's Not Enough

The Meetings in America III study commissioned by World-Com in 2001 found that seven out of ten of us work virtually. The age of the colocated team is dying. Working virtually is the new norm. People work virtually out of homes, customer sites, distant offices, and mobile settings (like airports or hotels). They're connecting across locations, cultures, companies, and languages to bring products and services to the global marketplace. One out of three either manage or are managed by people that perform their work somewhere else.

The greatest challenge facing people that work virtually, however, is to reduce travel. *USA Today* (March 16, 1999) reported on a National Business Travel Association study of 440 corporate travel managers. A whopping nine out of ten companies had initiatives to reduce travel. If anyone thinks that the mandate to reduce travel is a passing fad, think again. It's not. The facts are clear. In the present and future, teams that work virtually will travel significantly less than they do today.

> *The need for teams to evolve to Bionic eTeamwork isn't optional. It's a mandate for success.*

Why do virtual teams need to reduce travel? The people who hold the financial strings of our business usually get to answer first: reduce costs. The airlines have been merciless in extracting money from business travelers: high ticket prices, change and cancellation fees, and exorbitant overcharging in low-competition markets. Governments have acted without hesitation to tack taxes and fees onto hotel rooms, sometimes adding 20 to 30 percent onto the bill. Car rental companies have no shame about doubling the market cost of gasoline if the car is returned with a less than full tank, charging auto insurance rates that are higher than the daily rate of the car, and tacking on license plate and other fees (as if the rental car wasn't expensive enough already). Travel is expensive. It plays a critical role in all virtual teamwork. The future, however, is telling us that teams will have significantly fewer opportunities to travel.

There's an even more compelling reason to reduce travel. If you work in a virtual environment, you know what that reason is: saving time. Time is the one commodity that we all share equally. No one gets around it: 24 hours a day is all each of us gets. With over a decade of corporate restructuring and reorganizations, we work hard, for long hours, and consistently put our best efforts forward. If we complete an assignment early or suddenly have some unscheduled time because a meeting is cancelled at the last minute, we don't use that time to goof off. The WorldCom Meetings in America III study showed that people reinvest 61 percent of the time they save in other work-related activities.

> The future, however, is telling us that teams will have significantly fewer opportunities to travel.

Another reason we want to save time is for our life outside of work. We want more personal time to be with our families and friends, enjoy our favorite activities and pastimes, and take a few moments for quiet time. We need to get away from the pressure cooker work environment and stress-filled travel environment. We need respite through other aspects of our lives that recharge our spirit and our love of life. Personal time lets us get away from our work and recharge our batteries, so we can return to it refreshed, relaxed, and ready for the challenge ahead. Personal time is important for us and for our business.

So, if we can reduce the need to travel—without compromising the quality of the interaction—it's almost like buying time. The time we buy impacts both our business and personal lives. Take Eric, an engineer, who had traveled to Lake Tahoe for business. Like many people who work in a virtual environment, he had planned to stay the weekend to enjoy two days of skiing. With pain written all over his face, he described the skier's nirvana he was forced to leave early. He said, "The skiing conditions couldn't have been better. Fresh powder. Sunny skies. The midday air temperature was 30 degrees. It was the best skiing of the season." His trip was cut short because he had to attend an emergency meeting in his office in Georgia on Monday morning.

If Eric skied Saturday and flew back Sunday, "The airline wanted to rip me off for an additional $1,000." So, he had to fly back Saturday. The tragedy is that Eric wasn't Bionic. He had a cell phone and a laptop. But he didn't know about web conference technology, and he didn't know how to use it to meet as effectively in a digital space as he had been doing in a physical space. The cost to Eric was the frustration of losing two days of awesome skiing conditions. The cost to the team was a weekend delay in responding to the customer issue that had emerged the previous Friday.

This way of doing business is right out of Jurassic Park. Were Eric Bionic, he could have bought the time, solved the problem at light speed, and done it all, with days to spare!

> *If we can reduce the need to travel— without compromising the quality of the interaction— it's almost like buying time.*

Teams have more time-related challenges than reducing travel. Get revved up for the next wave: the HyperSpeed, complex, global e-marketplace. The pace of e-business, products, markets, customers, services, and communication—everything that virtual teams must do is about to soar into HyperSpeed.

For business in the high-tech era, HyperSpeed is already here. Take Kent Harmon, Director of R&D Effectiveness at Texas Instruments. He said, "In the 1980s, we measured product life cycles in years and product development in months. In the age of the Internet and wireless communications, we measure product life cycles in quarters, and product development in days." To collaborate at these speeds, teams need more than travel, e-mail, and conference calls. They need to know how to be Bionic.

HyperSpeed is required of a growing number of complex, global business teams. They are moving so fast across so many locations, travel is not an option at all. Take Laura Schmidthammer, a Development Manager at Alltel. Alltel does software development in the automobile finance industry.

> *Tomorrow's suc-*
> *cess is created by*
> *teams that have*
> *left their addiction*
> *to "place."*

Schmidthammer said, "Our team's challenge was to bring in a project with 150 people, with a staff in 24 cities, speaking 7 languages—on time. Moving people to one location wasn't an option for our team." They did it, with time to spare. The team's well practiced eCollaboration skills let them work at HyperSpeed on an immensely complex project. The bonus is that they were able to retain very, very valuable staff members in widely dispersed locations—some that would not have moved to Little Rock, Detroit, or anywhere else.

All of us have technology. It's no longer enough. Technology is merely the ante to get into the game. Tomorrow's success is created by teams that have left their addiction to "place" and have set new roots, new skills, and new practices in a whole new way of collaborating online.

Yes, indeed, we have the technology. We're wired with a universe of electronic wizardry that has *potential* to take us beyond a brave new world. The software and hardware companies of the world have laid a foundation, creating a new universe that boggles our imagination! The reality is, however, that virtual teams have hardly scratched the surface of how to collaborate in ways that build extraordinarily fast, cohesive eTeamwork. No wonder so many people want to hop on planes to be in one site! Those who rely mostly on e-mail and conference calls have metaphorically only put their foot in the water of new ways to connect and collaborate, from afar. Bionic eTeamwork changes all of that.

As such, many are caught in the two lower stages of virtual teamwork—the Disabled and Mechanical stages. In the Disabled stage, they feel their communication via technology keeps them from creating real teamwork and trust. They are the first to hop on a plane to hold an onsite meeting, so people can "really" communicate and feel a sense of team. In the Mechanical stage, people use technology and tolerate its shortcomings. They have not yet learned, however, how to embrace its power to collaborate in extraordinarily fast and cohesive ways, from afar.

The reality is that technology is just a tool. The magic only happens when people and teams master how to build trust, collaboration, and community across time zones and space, not just "place." We all must get very good in new best practices to extend our human touch, our human reach, and our human community in a virtual environment. People that communicate in Bionic ways know how to create that magic, and you can too. Being Bionic is a choice that comes with huge human and task rewards.

> *Communication in this new environment is not only effective— it's fun.*

Like it or not, technology is a part of our being. It's here to stay. There's no going back to "the good old days" of colocated teams, lavish travel budgets, and unpressured time. There's no more time to bury our heads in the sand, hoping that technology will stop advancing. Technology will move forward with even greater speed. We need to get very good at how we use it to connect on a human level.

In contrast, Bionic eTeams love their technology. They establish a close relationship with it, carefully learning and plotting the role the technology will play in making the group faster, stronger, and better. Then they create a plan to leverage its power to communicate, collaborate, and connect on a human level. Together with their Bionic parts, the team gets extraordinary work done from points all over the globe, near and far.

The bonus is that communication in this new environment is not only effective—it's fun. Yes, fun! Fun is important. Fun is laughter, playfulness, and camaraderie. It is the team enjoying the experience of working online together. Fun is also the creativity, problem solving, decision making, and interaction a team creates as it does its work. It is a level of fun in a digital space that is as delightful as what teams have created in a single physical space. It is the opposite of boring, passive conference calls where everyone is doing e-mail, only partly attending to the meeting.

Whether you lead an eTeam, are a member of an eTeam, or must collaborate with people that work somewhere else— *Bionic eTeamwork* is a book that is designed to take you to a fast, cohesive new way of working, from afar.

> Bionic teams don't just have technology, they know how to leverage it to build human rapport and results.

Being on the same e-mail system doesn't make a team. The next wave is Bionic eTeamwork—teams that don't just *have* technology, but that know how to *leverage it to build human rapport and results.* Yesterday's leadership best practices and today's mechanical communication practices won't take us far enough, fast enough. To be successful, eTeams must build a bridge to the next level: Bionic. Let's get started!

eTeam Evolution 2

Disabled, Mechanical, Bionic

> *A team that uses technology poorly has no advantage over a team that doesn't have that technology at all.*
> **Jim Kutsko**

According to Bill Gates, technology will change more in the next 10 years than it has in the previous 50. To stay on top of the technoblitz, companies roll out technology on very aggressive timelines. Unfortunately, however, they're so consumed about getting new technology out that they often forget about the people.

I am reminded of a vacation one businesswoman had in London a few years ago. She was waiting for a bus to take her from a suburb of London to Piccadilly Circus, in the heart of town. As she saw the bus approaching, she stepped to the curb. The bus, half full of people, drove right by her, as if she were invisible. A few minutes later, another bus pulled up at the same curb. When the driver opened the door, the businesswoman explained what happened. The driver responded, "Well, if the last driver stopped to pick you up, he might have been late!"

Technology has been rolled out so fast in companies all over the world that many people feel like they've been left standing at a metaphorical curb. New software, new upgrades, new features—an endless list of new technologies promises to make us better, faster, and stronger. Although we all recognize technology's promise, many of us are jaded because we just don't have any time to integrate it into how we do our work. The best we have seen is only a partial delivery of the promise to make us more productive and effective.

Take one senior manager who was promoted one step up in his company, to director level. One week after the promotion, a box shows up on his desk. Inside the box was a brand new pager—a super deluxe model. Slightly larger than a normal pager, it looked like a pager on steroids. It had a little cover that opened to expose a minikeyboard that could send and receive e-mail messages. Plus, it had quite a few additional features, such as voice message notification and stock quotes.

> *Today's teamwork, however, requires a level of human assimilation and human sophistication with technology that can't be learned on the fly.*

Now, this director already had a text pager that worked just fine for his needs. He said, "I didn't know if the new pager was sent to me by my boss or the IT department. The technology just suddenly appeared on my desk. It was not tied to any strategy to make me more effective, productive, or trustworthy as a leader in the organization. It did, however, come with a 200-page booklet that I knew I didn't have time to read."

There was a time when people had the time to experiment with new technology, to learn it "when they had some extra time." Today's teamwork, however, requires a level of human assimilation and human sophistication with technology that can't be learned on the fly. The technology just keeps on coming, but the "big payoff" for many still hasn't happened. The problem isn't the technology. Today's technology can do just about anything you want it to do. The problem, instead, is on the people side of *integrating* technology. The spark that enables technology to create real magic in dispersed groups comes from the human side. Without the human element, there's no spark, no magic, and no real connection.

The name of the game to reach high performance in the third millennium is not just that teams evolve, but that they evolve faster than the rest. They have to build trust faster, make decisions faster, get aligned faster, and produce faster—all while linked from locations dotting the globe.

What's the alternative? Teams that fail to evolve fast enough will fail to compete. Metaphorically, you can't compete with Steve Austin unless you become Bionic like Steve Austin.

All of us who communicate virtually have to be smarter about how to leverage technology not just to send and receive messages, but also to extend our human touch and increase team speed, virtually. We need to embrace collaborative technology, and use it to collaborate, not give slide shows to one another. We have to learn new skills for how to build and align an interactive, close community of people who don't share the same physical space. Lastly, we must master how to grow the team's human connection and trust when people aren't in one place.

The greatest challenge is to do all of these at breakneck speed, significantly faster than we have ever done them before. When we do, we're Bionic. When we are Bionic, we're not just at the cutting edge, or even just a cut above the others. We'll be light years ahead of our competition. We won't have to work until midnight because everyone on our eTeam is smarter about how to succeed in this new world of eTeamwork.

eTeams go through three predictable phases in their quest to evolve to high-performance eTeamwork. This model will help you identify your eTeam's and your own evolution to Bionic. Subsequent chapters will point out how to become exponentially better, faster, and stronger as a team.

1. The Disabled Phase

2. The Mechanical Phase

3. The Bionic Phase

Let's take a brief look at each. And then we'll look at what you and your eTeam need to do to evolve to the highest level: Bionic eTeamwork.

▓ Evolution Phase #1: Disabled

The first, and least effective, phase of eTeamwork is the Disabled Phase.

In the Disabled Phase, people are disarmed by technology. The only environment in which they are comfortable communicating is face to face, in the same physical location. As a result, they consider any communication through technology as a dramatically inferior option. They feel disabled from creating relationships successfully, accomplishing work, or feeling any degree of trust unless people are in the same room.

One distinction is critical. Travel doesn't make a leader, team, or individual disabled in a virtual environment. Most virtual teamwork requires some travel so that people can get to know one another, build their relationships, and work through some critical details about the work. The factor that traps people in the Disabled Phase is the *mandate* to travel to feel trust, work through issues, and get "real work" done.

Teams in the Disabled Phase consistently show four key symptoms.

1. Constant, Heavy Travel

If the team needs to make an important decision, people travel. If the leader wants to realign the team's work, people travel. If the team needs to collaborate, people travel.

People that are caught in the Disabled Phase are the first ones to hop on a plane or drive across town to talk face to face, rather than collaborate through technology, like e-mail or conference calls. In global business, these teams are disabled because they rely too much on being in one location to get any work done together.

Take Hal, an information technology (IT) manager. He led a team that had a primary location on each side of the Atlantic Ocean—one in the United Kingdom and the other in the United States. Two companies had merged, and his team's mission was to integrate the computer system of each former company into one. For the new company to be successful launching their product in the world marketplace, they had to be able to share, coordinate, and collaborate on research and development worldwide. Choosing the right products and tools, as well as integrating the computer systems into one, were critical.

As leader of this two-continent eTeam, Hal made so many flights across the ocean that he earned his way into the most elite of the elite status frequent flier programs—on two airlines. For two years, he alternated two weeks in the United Kingdom with two weeks in the United States. Although he did use e-mail, voice mail, and the phone to communicate, he always gravitated to the face-to-face mode (through travel) for every important decision, commitment, or interaction.

Teams that span languages and cultures usually need to travel more than teams that don't. Some of the travel at the beginning can be frequent and heavy. In Hal's case, his travel schedule never diminished. It stayed the same for two years, which was stressful to the team and to his family. The team resented that they could never get a hold of him when he wasn't

> *Teams that span languages and cultures usually need to travel more than teams that don't.*

at their site. His family resented that he was never home, even when he was in town. In fact, his wife had filed for a divorce.

Hal wasn't the only one that relied too much on travel to get real work done. One consultant's report showed that there were weeks when 50 people at a time were on a plane traveling across the ocean—all at business class fares. The company couldn't sustain that expense and cracked down. Others who used to travel before the crackdown now complained loudly, saying that they just couldn't get their work done. People on both sides of the ocean were openly complaining about the reduced travel, pining to return "to the good old days" of having everyone work in one location.

2. A Compelling Need to Be Face to Face to See What Was Going On

Hal and the team had another critical reason to travel so frequently. Everyone felt a high need to physically see and track what was going on. Hal said, "Colocated teams work well. But I just can't trust that people who work out of my view will really get things done right." Hal had the same frustration as everyone else. Sometimes the work was delivered as expected, sometimes not. At still other times, it was not delivered at all.

Of a larger concern to all was missed water-cooler talk that is so important for teamwork.

Of a larger concern to all was missed water-cooler talk that is so important for teamwork. Water-cooler talk refers to informal conversations that give people a pulse on issues, challenges, and people's lives. They are also opportunities for people to create personal relationships, exchange personal information, and provide immediate support to each other. Water-cooler conversations can take place in the hallway, by the coffee machine, in the cafeteria, in any environment before or after work, or, naturally, at the water cooler. They happen throughout the day and give each participant the feeling of being "in the know."

People on each side of the ocean had their own water-cooler conversations, but the team had created no substitute from afar, except to travel to participate firsthand. Travel was the only way team members could capture a fraction of water-cooler talk. Like playing the lottery, each hoped they were present when an important nugget came to light.

As a result, the team constantly worked in crisis mode. While Hal was in the United Kingdom, one of his key people in the United States unexpectedly quit. "I had a meeting with her about ten days ago, and she didn't say a thing to me. Today, I received an e-mail tendering her resignation. I had no idea that she was even considering leaving." Hal gambled that he would be at the water cooler at the right time. He lost. Had he paid more attention to creating real relationships with his key people—instead of checking up on them all the time—he would have improved his odds of being "in the know."

A water-cooler conversation might have given Hal warning signs, but their weak relationship gave him no signs and no warning, from afar.

3. Team Collaborative Technology Isn't in Their Thought Pattern or Team Process

Even though Hal's official title was Technology Integration Team Leader, he really didn't lead a single team. He led two separate teams that just happened to work about 5,000 miles apart. Before the team was chartered, the U.K. and U.S. organizations were completely separate. Each was well entrenched in its own technologies, processes, and methods to manage an enormous database of research findings. This team's purpose was to create a new and better system than either of the former systems. Combining these research capabilities was an enormous undertaking, but mandatory for leveraging research findings globally.

This team had plenty of team camaraderie and teamwork in each separate location; little to none, from afar. People at the U.S. location had bonded. People at the U.K. location had bonded. But their bonding didn't cross the ocean.

In a face-to-face setting, everyone appeared warm and pleasant to each other. In reality, though, people from the opposite location were always outsiders. None felt they had the relationships to address the real issues that were dividing this team. The U.K. people felt that the U.S. people were imposing a U.S. approach on them. The U.S. people felt that the U.K. people were closeminded and unwilling to compromise.

> *People from the opposite location were always outsiders. None felt they had the relationships to address the real issues that were dividing this team.*

Instead of a team that created an exceptional result, inspiring everyone in both locations, they had a group of people that achieved only a small part of their potential. They believed they couldn't be a team, and they weren't. Like the plumber that has a house full of stopped-up drains, this technology team—the experts in technology for their company—failed to apply technology creatively to build teamwork across the ocean. Their focus on information over-shadowed their need to focus on team collaboration and real trust.

Colocated teams sometimes get caught unaware when they migrate to a virtual environment. Take Alexandra, a corporate vice president for a Silicon Valley–based dot-com. Over a weekend in January 2001, the company had moved into its brand new office building. First thing Monday morning, Alexandra had a 7 AM meeting scheduled in the executive conference room. A committee had designed this room to every detail, including the executive meeting table, the plush executive chairs, and even the global-theme pictures on the wall. About five minutes before meeting time, Alexandra rushed into the meeting room. She looked for a speakerphone so she could conference with her partners in Atlanta and London. There was none. She looked for a phone. There was none. She looked for a phone jack. You guessed it: none. She looked for a port to link her computer to the network. None, again.

The people on the meeting room design committee always met face to face. Communicating globally from this room wasn't in their thought pattern. No one even thought about linking people in the room to the rest of the world.

4. They Are Stuck on Methods That Are Designed for Face-to-Face Teamwork

Hal had led several very successful same-site teams. He had a natural ability to make people feel comfortable. When he was on site, people could see his passion for his work. He used that time to talk vision, reward and recognize his people, and move work forward. Every other two weeks, however, when he was on the other side of the ocean, the spark was gone. People reverted back to their old habits and attitudes.

Only 15 years ago, Tom Peters revolutionized leadership communication around the world with Management by Wandering/Walking Around (MBWA). The technique was designed to get leaders to walk out of their offices and communicate with their team on a very human level. The focus of the communication was to talk vision, coach people for success, and catch people doing things right. The strategy was profoundly powerful, and leaders around the world embraced it.

If you're an MBWA diehard follower like Hal, however, here's the problem. MBWA is a strategy that is designed for a different time in the evolution of teamwork. Today's teams aren't just outside your door. Instead, people are spread out all over the world. With eTeams, face-to-face time is too rare to be the primary communication vehicle. If MBWA is the core way you lead, a strategy that caused you so much success only a few years ago will now keep you and your team from evolving to Bionic.

> *No one even thought about linking people in the room to the rest of the world.*

Travel is important in all eTeams, especially up front. But a team is disabled if decisions, trust, alignment, and other "real" communication have to wait for the next face-to-face meeting.

How You Know Your Team Is in the Disabled Phase

- Constant travel, because a face-to-face meeting is the only way the leader feels she can know what is really going on.

- Decisions and action are postponed until the next face-to-face visit.

- Low levels of trust and rapport, especially when people are distant.

- The best or most sought-after assignments go to the people who work right outside the leader's door.

- Members are unable to trust people or work that can't be seen.

- Technophobia—people resist or fear computers and/or communication technology.
- Face to face is the only way groups can collaborate effectively and get work done.

■ Evolution Phase #2: Mechanical

The second, and most common, phase of eTeamwork is the Mechanical Phase.

> *In the Mechanical Phase, people have a technical connection, but they're really out of touch on a human level.*

In the Mechanical Phase, people have a technical connection, but they're really out of touch on a human level when they are not in the same place. They accept technology and sometimes find an advantage in it. Generally, though, they feel disconnected on a personal level from the people they communicate with in a virtual environment every day. In this phase, when people communicate through technology, the message frequently gets mutated, often leaving others feeling cold, excluded, and confused.

Take conference calls. One of my favorite cartoons from *The Wall Street Journal* shows three people standing around a speakerphone. Each is making a nasty face or a nasty hand gesture toward the phone. The caption under the cartoon says, "They really *are* doing what you think they are doing on the other side of your speakerphone conference call." We've all been there. The speakerphone relays our voice, but little else. The result is human communication that carries speech, but most of its humanity has been stripped away.

Teams in the Mechanical Phase consistently show five key symptoms.

1. eCommunication Feels Impersonal

In the Mechanical Phase, people accept that they must substitute mechanical communication for traditional, warmer human communication. They say goodbye to spontaneous conversations with people at the water cooler down the hall. Now hundreds of e-mail messages, dozens of voice mail messages, and endless boring conference calls replace a key way they've communicated for years.

In fact, people learn to tolerate the impersonal nature of communication through electronic media. Take one client who complained about *drive-by e-mail* messages. The term caught me by surprise, so I asked her to define drive-by e-mail. She said, "People will write things in e-mail messages that they would never say to you face to face. We call them drive-by e-mails because they're like what people do in their cars. People that don't know each other communicate in ways that seem rude, offensive, and cold."

Some people in the Mechanical Phase try to find ways to make the message more human (like ☺ or :) emoticons). But in truth, they know this: although eCommunication has advantages, in the Mechanical Phase it just doesn't feel as personal, open, or effective as face to face.

When eCommunication feels so impersonal, an almost predictable change occurs in how people communicate through e-mail. Somehow using e-mail to "make sure everyone is informed" gets morphed into "make sure I don't get blamed." Processing the messages in your in-box gets transformed into the game of e-mail musical chairs: Don't get caught holding the e-mail action item when the music stops (a problem occurs). To win the game, get it out of your electronic in-basket—in writing—so that the problem is someone else's fault. Best of all, you can produce the paper trail to prove it, complete with time and date stamp!

2. People Feel Overwhelmed

In the Mechanical Phase, the volume of eCommunication that comes at people each day is overwhelming. Take one leader who went on vacation for two weeks. When she returned, she had over 1,000 e-mail messages waiting for her! Or another that said, "I am overwhelmed by e-mail. When I arrive at work in the morning, I have a clear idea of what I need to complete that day. Then I check my e-mail, and I am sent in fifty other directions with "urgent" this's and "must have" that's. Before I know it, the time is 4 PM, and I still haven't begun the work I set for myself at the beginning of the day." The team that wants to be proactive becomes reactive under the weight of too many e-mails that become the priority and pull people off task.

> *The team that wants to be proactive becomes reactive under the weight of too many e-mails that become the priority and pull people off task.*

The overwhelming volume of messages causes other predictable problems. People are frustrated that they can't get the responsiveness they need to their e-messages. Many say that they just don't have the relationships to get a response. Across distance, they also don't have the power. Take one engineer who said, "I hate sending a message to HR because they never respond. I had to get a class approved for reimbursement by someone who works 1,000 miles away from me. Despite all my e-mail and voice mail messages, it took two weeks to get a response, which was too late. If that person worked in the next building, I would have walked to his desk, found him, stood over his desk, and waited for the signature right then and there. As it was, I had no choice but to keep sending messages into the abyss."

3. Impact on Recipients Is Not a Priority; Firing Out Messages Is

In the Mechanical Phase, frequently little thought is given to the impact of a message that is sent to distant others. These e-mail offenders send anything to everyone with little consequence. They usually work in the seven out of ten organizations that have no clear written norms or policies that protect people from e-mail abuse.

Take the speed bump story. After hours, one building of a high-tech company repaved its parking lot, adding speed bumps for safety. The contractor had not yet painted the lines for the parking spaces or the speed bumps. One of the first employees to the building the following morning drove too fast into the lot. In the presunrise darkness, she couldn't see any obvious changes. She hit the unexpected speed bump way too fast and bashed the bottom of her brand new car.

Angry, she went straight to her desk and fired off an e-mail. Although her building had only about 200 people, the message went to a distribution list of all 10,000 company employees that worked in Silicon Valley. Later that morning, as all 10,000 recipients fired off either angry or supportive responses to the distribution list, the entire computer network came to a grinding halt. For four hours, no one in the company had access to his computer, e-mails, or files. In a flash, one short e-mail about a speed bump directly created 40,000 unproductive work hours—the equivalent of 20 full-time employees for one year.

4. Out of Sight, Out of Mind

The transition from a colocated team mindset to a virtual team mindset is filled with landmines. Teams have the technology to communicate with people that are everywhere in the world. With the touch of a key, we send and receive e-mails from all over the world. With our phones, we can talk with just about anyone, anywhere on the planet, and beyond. We have the technology. But we are still caught in the twilight zone between here, there, or everywhere.

Take Shantelle. She led a team of nine in Dallas and one in Switzerland. Hans dialed in for the weekly meeting, linking to Shantelle and the other eight people who sat in the room with her. Shantelle always sent out an agenda by e-mail before the meeting. Whenever she had to make a last-minute change in the agenda, she gave a paper copy of it to the eight people in Dallas at the beginning of the meeting. When Hans asked for a copy, one of the Dallas team members volunteered to fax it to him. The problem was that the fax number was for the office. The meeting was at 8 PM in Zurich, and Hans was already home. During the meeting itself, the Dallas members passed documents back and forth that Hans could not receive, wrote on a flip chart that Hans could not see, and had discussions that Hans rarely had an opportunity to participate in.

This brief story relays a simple but very common occurrence in virtual meetings: out of sight, out of mind. This team proudly described itself as global team. They weren't. The real team and the only teamwork were "here" in Dallas. Hans was "there" in Switzerland. What they needed was to be "everywhere." Because of this team's technology choice and approach, Hans was cast in the unfortunate role of being out of sight, out of mind. It was unfortunate for Hans, because no one likes to feel like the forgotten stepchild. It was unfortunate for the team, because his key value was untapped. It was unfortunate for teamwork, because the interaction was driven by place.

5. The Power of Technology Is Largely Untapped

Take Brian, a company president, who was talking about his cell phone. Passing it like a hockey puck across the conference table to me, he said, "Look at this powerful tool. It's not just a cell phone. It has a pager, a calculator, an address book, and dozens of other features that I don't even know about. But it's like every other technology product in my world. I am probably using only one tenth of its power to make me more productive."

The rapid stream of new technology overwhelms people. The result: technology's power is largely untapped. One leading oil and gas company was about to introduce desktop video teleconferencing and Microsoft's NetMeeting (one of many collaborative Web technologies) at every computer station companywide. The IT leadership was proactive about providing technology training to help raise skill levels.

The pilot course to roll out this new technology, however, was another trip through the Twilight Zone. The instructor said, "NetMeeting is a hands-on computer technology, and the pilot program was a hands-on work33shop. I couldn't get anyone to touch the keys on the keyboard. It was almost as though if people touched a key, that now they were forced to use yet another technology to communicate. They clearly were not interested in doing that."

After the break, the instructor confronted the class. Finally, someone raised her hand and said, "Before we learn all of this advanced technology, can't we just learn how to change our voice mail greetings?"

Web conference technology is one of the most important technologies for virtual teams since the introduction of the phone, conference calls, and e-mail. It enables a virtual team to create an online meeting space that rivals the traditional small meeting room down the hall. With Web conferencing, teams can quickly share documents, partici-pate in live team polling, create dia-grams on a live whiteboard, brainstorm in a live chat, go on a live Web tour to-gether, and muchmore. (See <www.bi onicteam.com> for an illustrated tour of PlaceWare, WebEx, NetMeeting, Sametime, CentraNow, and other top Web con-ference technologies.)

> *Web conference technology is one of the most impor-tant technologies for virtual teams since the introduc-tion of the phone, conference calls, and e-mail.*

People flock to this new tool, use it for a while, find little value, and then stop using it. No wonder they want their travel budgets back. The problem isn't Web conference technology. It is the way people use it.

In the Mechanical Phase, people use Web conference technology for "show and tell" presentations. Interaction is minimal—maybe a poll every five minutes that may or may not be related to the topic. Web conference technology does show and tell well, but that's not enough to keep a virtual team en-gaged from the desktop. Speeding continuous team interac-tion is its real power. In the Mechanical Phase, people are more concerned about sharing information than collaborating. Sharing information is a trap of the Mechanical Phase. Online team collaboration is the future.

> *Sharing information is a trap of the Mechanical Phase. Online team collaboration is the future.*

The power of the technology is also untapped because teams haven't made the critical connection with how to leverage it to be dramatically more effective and productive. Unfortunately, neither have most organizations. They buy technology without a clear strategy to make it not just a substitute or an aide, but *a tool HUMANS will use to speed decision making, team collaboration, and sense of team—in exponential leaps.*

Take one leader who complained about how his electronic teamroom failed to inspire his Asian virtual team to collaborate. Ron, the leader of the team, lamented, "I expected it to be used constantly by my team, to make it a central place for my people to create high performance as a team. In less than one month, it has turned into a document graveyard. No one uses it, and no one is collaborating. It didn't help my team one bit." Ron's problem wasn't electronic teamroom technology, but his mechanical approach to using it. People don't go to a file cabinet to be inspired or connected. That's his job. In the Mechanical Phase, leaders will continue to be disillusioned until they handle the human factor first, and then add the technology that makes life better for the people.

Electronic teamrooms are as important to virtual teamwork as is Web conference technology. Sometimes designed with warm, friendly graphics, electronic teamrooms provide a common online place from which worldwide teams can easily connect with or collaborate on critical team documents. The better teamrooms also enable version control, annotation capability, reminder notices, and tracking control, among other features. (See <www.bionicteam.com> for more information about eRoom, Exchange 2000 Collaboration tools, and other technologies.) The technology is only as effective as the way people use it. In the Mechanical Phase, teams fail to establish relationships first, and see the electronic teamroom as a key way to build the relationship, not just exchange documents, from afar.

The fact is that technology is advancing at the speed of light. Most companies have done a poor job of implementing technology, largely because the people side is secondary, not primary. In the Mechanical Phase, people want to upgrade their basic skills. With the colocatepace of business today, however, they have no time to "discover" it themselves.

In the Mechanical Phase, they clumsily choose the wrong media for the message, sending trust and results tripping flat on their face. Because no one can trust that the message will be received, people overreact. They send the same message via too many different media—like e-mail, fax, and pagers—adding to everyone's stack with little consideration for the time and priorities of the recipient.

I remember one leader who remarked how much he hated the day when the *Harvard Business Review* came out. Now the *Harvard Business Review* is one of my favorite business periodicals. So I asked him the inevitable next question: Why? The leader said, "The company always wanted to be at the top of their game. So when the *Harvard Business Review* came out and some executive read some article, suddenly a brand new program was immediately rolled out throughout the entire company.

The problem was that interest in that program, and attention focused on that program, lasted only a very short time—usually only until the next issue came out. Then the cycle repeated itself again."

Teams caught in the Mechanical Phase are very much like the leader just described. Someone learns about a new technology, and then millions are invested rolling out that technology—supposedly to enable the organization to stay at the top of their game. Only some of that technology delivers only some of its power.

In the Mechanical Phase, however, the people have not really assimilated technology, largely because the people side of using it to collaborate faster or build relationships from afar has been left out of the picture. The assumption is that because technology is so simple and intuitive, people will pick it up. In the Mechanical Phase, they don't. They're too busy digging through their endless stack of e-mail.

> *The assumption is that because technology is so simple and intuitive, people will pick it up. In the Mechanical Phase, they don't.*

Throwing technology at a communication problem doesn't solve that communication problem. Teams will stay in the Mechanical Phase until they, and their companies, satisfy the human side of assimilating technology. The only way to progress out of this phase is to rethink how they use technology to connect as a team on a human level. They must reinvent how they use technology to become fast and cohesive. Then they must add resources to support a new way of collaborating, virtually.

How You Know Your Team Is in the Mechanical Phase

- A strong sense of "out of the loop, out of the group."
- "Out of control" volumes of communication.
- Low levels of collaboration across locations, usually because cross-site collaboration is too slow and frustrating.
- Conference calls are a good time to do e-mail.
- Reactive, not proactive, focus.
- Little to no sense of team.
- A show-and-tell approach to online meetings and presentations, creating a passive state for those linked to the meeting.
- Team eMeetings are held when convenient for the people at the eLeader's site, with little regard to time considerations (having to meet over lunch, linking to meetings outside business hours in your time zone) of other sites.
- A last-minute scramble always happens around conference calls to send documents or a revised agenda to people at "remote" sites.

■ Evolution Phase #3: Bionic

The third, and most effective, phase of eTeamwork is the Bionic Phase.

In the Bionic Phase, technology is not a hindrance. It's an accelerator. Bionic eTeams use technology in ways that accelerate team rapport *and* team results, simultaneously. Technology isn't a last choice—or even an alternate choice—for communication. It's the first choice, because people use it to extend their human power and capability.

Remember that with his Bionic legs, Steve Austin could run ten times faster than people with human legs. With his Bionic parts, he was infinitely more capable of attaining his human goals than without them. Teams that master how to be Bionic tap into that same kind of power. Like a scientist who uses the computer to enhance human brainpower to understand DNA faster, Bionic eTeams use technology purposefully to extend their ability to connect faster, on both human and task levels.

> *Teams will stay in the Mechanical Phase until they, and their companies, satisfy the human side of assimilating technology.*

It doesn't matter whether people use common technology or newer groupware. Human performance and human rapport are at the heart of how Bionic eTeams use the technology. For Bionic eTeams, technology doesn't replace the human process. Rather, *the way people use technology enhances the human process.* Bionic eTeams use technology to extend their human reach, their human touch, and their human capability.

Bionic eTeamwork with New Technology

Take the Global Environment, Health & Safety (EH&S) Work Process Implementation Team at Dow Chemical. The team was created to roll out a global process that would improve Dow's EH&S performance. With a lean EH&S organization of 1,100 people spread across 132 sites, speaking 12 languages, and operating with 40 percent fewer people, this was no small task. What a paradox! At a time when the organization had no people to spare, it had to change faster, and with fewer resources than ever before—worldwide.

> For Bionic eTeams, technology doesn't replace the human process. Rather, the way people use technology enhances the human process.

The Process Implementation Team was a small group whose members worked from such far-flung places as Germany, The Netherlands, Brazil, Australia, Canada, and Midland (Michigan). The team represented three parts of the organization: expertise, manufacturing, and business. Had this team chosen the traditional approach to create and roll out a new process, their work would have taken five years—time they didn't have.

The traditional method wasn't an option because:

- *It was too slow.* In an aligned, global organization, implementation had to occur in one year, not five, worldwide. Suddenly, it was no longer satisfactory for change to trickle out to 132 sites, one at a time—Canada this month, Brazil next month, then Australia and other points beyond in the months that followed.

- *It was too locationcentric.* A process change in one place (like Hong Kong) impacts other people in other sites (like São Paulo). It was no longer acceptable to roll out change in ways that have people in different locations using different processes. Instead, the rollout needed to occur simultaneously, worldwide.

- *It was too costly.* The cost involved more than expensive transocean airline travel. It also involved human cost: thousands of unproductive, mind-numbing trips across multiple time zones; time ripped away from family and local communities; and time delay in making decisions and moving forward as a team.

So, the Process Implementation Team chose the Bionic route. They completed the work in 10 months (not 60), cutting the time to implementation by an amazing 83 percent. With full buy-in by everyone on the team, they put in place and trained people worldwide on a whole new work process that had a $50 million impact on the company. Because the team never met each other physically when doing the work, they saved the company an estimated $200,000 in travel costs alone. Best of all, the team felt great about its interaction and its results. This worldwide team suffered no lack of team spirit or results.

> *They made a conscious decision not to let distance or technology constrain them from being a real team in every sense of the word.*

How did they do it? This team's best practices echo those of others that have learned to operate at HyperSpeed. Let's look at the specifics.

1. From the Beginning, the Team Made a Conscious Decision to "Be One Global Team"

Many teams that work in a virtual environment feel that they can't be a real team unless they travel and do the work on location. That is why the Dow team's first step is so critical. Actually just about every team you'll read about in this book began with this crucial first step. They made a conscious decision not to let distance or technology constrain them from being a real team in every sense of the word. They accepted no compromise in the level of teamwork they could create together, from afar. And then they became very creative in how they built and reinforced real teamwork throughout their team's work.

The Dow team knew that teamwork wasn't about sending volumes of e-mail to each other or listening passively to conference calls. Quite the contrary. Teamwork is a very active and participative process where humans interact together, make decisions together, and rely on each other, spontaneously. It's a highly collaborative process where the team charts new territory together, resolves problems together, and gets things done together that make people feel good. It is about creating human trust and a human community that binds people to each other and to their important work. The technology, and more importantly the human best practices that the Dow team employed, enabled real teamwork without the need to travel.

2. The Leader Supplemented Conference Calls with Web Conference Technology

> Teamwork is a very active and partici-pative process where humans interact together, make decisions together, and rely on each other, spontaneously.

Did you ever play the game as a child where several people sit in a line or cir-cle? The first person relays a verbal message to the second, then the sec-ond relays the message to a third, and so on, one at a time. The process con-tinues until the last person in the line has heard it. The last person then is required to say the message out loud to the others. If you ever played this game, you know that the last message is often severely distorted, sometimes unrecognizable from the first.

The same distortion happens in conference calls when your team works from individual copies of a spreadsheet, crafts an agreement, brainstorms a solution, or discusses an issue with words alone. Each person has a different interpre-tation of exactly what was said, agreed to, or decided. So the issue gets revisited again at the next meeting.

The communication the Dow team had to manage was infinitely more complex. The leader could have sent out a spreadsheet by e-mail for everyone to keep his or her copy of the process, agreement, or discussion. However, everyone would have had a different picture and a different understand-ing. The team would have experienced similar confusion, miscommunication, and message distortion as in the game mentioned previously.

The leader never could have achieved the team's objectives with conference call technology by itself. Their work was far too complex for a technology that is designed to relay only minimal communication cues. So Greg Dickson, the team leader, supplemented the conference call with an essential second tool—Web conference technology.

Dickson guided the team to create the implementation plan dynamically together using Web conference technology. (Please visit our Web site <www.bionicteam.com>, which overviews the top Web conference providers and tools in the industry, including pictures, details, and recommended uses for each.)

Without question, Web conference technology is a breakthrough technology that every virtual team needs. Web conferencing doesn't eliminate the need for travel. When used well, however, it dramatically reduces the need to travel. Although each Web conference option has its own advantages, here are some of the key features that enable Bionic eTeamwork:

- *Shared live applications and documents,* such as spreadsheets, Word documents, or Lotus Freelance presentations.

- *Shared keyboard control or meeting control,* to enable quick passing of full keyboard and mouse control to anyone in your eMeeting.

- *Live annotations,* so people can point, draw, and otherwise mark anything they see on screen. Some whiteboarding capability only lets the meeting leader have annotation power, while others give everyone that capability.

- *Live polling,* to enable live anonymous assessment of choices, decisions, and other meeting necessities.

- *Live chat,* to enable live polling, brainstorming, and more through words. Live chat input is normally not anonymous.

Dickson's team used Microsoft's NetMeeting Web conference technology. NetMeeting allowed each team member to view the same live spreadsheet, online. While the team talked through the conference call, they generated and viewed the implementation plan together on the shared-screen spreadsheet. At each team member's desktop in separate locations that dotted the world, each saw the same live document, the same changes, and the same highlighting in real time, during the global team meeting. Control of the online document was easily passed around the world, so that everyone could easily contribute—and did contribute—on many levels to the result.

Dow's Implementation Team could not have achieved its extraordinary result in such a short time with conference calls and long distance travel. Even though the team members circled the world, they used technology to create the human energy, spontaneity, and interaction of the "small meeting room down the hall." They felt like a team, acted like a team, and produced a $50 million solution in one-sixth the time a less unified team would have needed. That's Bionic eTeamwork!

3. The Team Created Teamwork Onscreen by the Way They Used Web Conference Technology

The fact that the team used Web conference technology did not go far enough. It was the HUMANware™ that Greg Dickson added that truly transformed this virtual team into a Bionic eTeam.

How did he do it?

He intentionally used technology in ways that built real teamwork, real collaboration, and real results onscreen. The emphasis was not on showing and telling. It was on collaboration, without compromise. He planned the meeting so people could see teamwork unfold on screen.

Heather Dixon, a member of the team, related one way Dickson created teamwork onscreen. "All of us could see a spreadsheet onscreen, live, in NetMeeting. The spreadsheet showed not just the data, but also the relationships. As we discussed the changes, then input them live on the spreadsheet, everyone at every site could see how one change in one site impacted other sites, and of course the other team members on the call. We immediately talked about issues and resolved them as a single global team."

She also talked about the team's Action Register. The Action Register was another spreadsheet that listed and tracked all action items. The Action Register was shared live via NetMeeting so everyone could see it, add to it, and mark items as complete. Dickson said, "It generated a lot of team spirit to see how much we were getting done week after week, all over the world."

> *The emphasis was not on showing and telling. It was on collaboration, without compromise.*

Lastly, Dixon said, "Everyone put his or her hand on everything we did. That's why it worked." No one was in idle mode. Greg Dickson created an environment for high participation on many levels. In fact, the real fun is discovering how many levels of relevant participation people can create online when they use Web conference technology in Bionic eTeamwork ways.

The Dow EH&S team created Bionic eTeamwork in their digital space. Their team spirit was no accident. They took the time to create it for themselves and discovered a whole new way to get connected from afar. This team completed its task with a worldwide celebration of the change. They created and sent a Party in a Tube to every location to launch the initiation in a fun, memorable way, during each site's workday all over the globe. Filled with balloons, posters, and a celebration plan, Party in a Tube marked the end of the old process and the beginning of the new. That's Bionic eTeamwork!

Bionic eTeamwork with Common Technology

Bionic eTeamwork does require teams to expand the number of technologies they use. Every Bionic eTeam needs to learn and get very comfortable with a number of Web collaboration technologies, like the one just mentioned.

> Bionic eTeams use technology to extend their human touch and human reach, virtually.

Teams can also create Bionic eTeamwork with other widely used technologies, such as cell phones, e-mail, and voice mail. The factor that lets any technology create Bionic eTeamwork is how people use the tool to extend their human touch and human reach, virtually.

Take Alan, a sales representative. As he took the seat next to me on a plane, I couldn't help but notice that he was smiling. Even after he settled in, shoving his attaché under the seat in front of him, he still was wearing that same smile. I couldn't resist commenting, "It looks like you are having a great day." Just as Alan looked back at me confirming that he was, his pager beeped. He took the pager off his belt and read the message that had just appeared in the text screen.

His smile turned into an even bigger grin, as he looked at me and said, "This has been an awesome day. I just sold a million dollar contract that I have been working on for months." Then he showed me the message on his pager. It was from the company CEO congratulating him on the sale and asking Alan to call him in the morning. The CEO wanted to know all about it. Alan was so pumped, he was ready to go do it again, even better!

As I continued to talk further with Alan, it was clear that his team's use of the pager was Bionic. The pager wasn't used to tell the representative that someone just sent him a fax. Instead, it was part of the communication plan that the mobile sales team had developed to keep its people motivated, anywhere, anytime.

Leadership 101 teaches leaders that the faster you can reward and recognize your people, the more powerful its impact. If the leader's eye is also focused on the bottom line, the fewer resources it takes to motivate people. When the contract was signed, Alan immediately submitted the electronic order, which automatically notified his boss and the CEO, who each immediately sent a personalized and spontaneous "congratulations" message on the pager.

The way that Alan's team used the pager was Bionic. The team built a specific plan about using technology to create and build a highly motivated work environment not bound by "place." The pager wasn't used to relay information. Instead, the leader used it to build momentum—*in the moment,* anywhere, anytime.

So Bionic eTeamwork is not about technology. Technology will always be in the picture. Bionic eTeamwork is about how people use technology to motivate, involve, and interact in very human ways.

> *In the Bionic Phase, eCommunication is streamlined, focused and purposeful—all clearly targeted to satisfy our human need to build rapport and results, exceptionally fast.*

Bionic eTeamwork Summary

Bionic eTeams move nimbly and swiftly through the virtual performance maze. They embrace third-generation collaborative tools, including Web conferencing, electronic teamrooms, and other collaborative technologies; then they use them to collaborate at HyperSpeed. They know how to give the right technology the human touch that propels them forward with immense speed and effectiveness.

As a result, Bionic eTeams make decisions faster, build consensus faster, build alignment faster, and collaborate at dramatically higher levels than traditional teams. In Bionic eTeams, momentum, participation, and interaction are constantly at high levels, never bound by location or time zones.

To do that, Bionic eTeams aren't slaves to the whim and uncoordinated priorities of thousands of e-mails, like in the Mechanical Phase. Quite the contrary. In the Bionic Phase, eCommunication is streamlined, focused, and purposeful—all clearly targeted to satisfy our human need to build rapport and results, exceptionally fast. Regardless of location or time zone, Bionic eTeams use technology to enhance their humanity: to keep momentum, participation, and interaction high.

How You Know Your Team Is in the Bionic Phase

- High sense of team on both task and emotional levels when working virtually.

- High degree of trust, rapport, and excitement, which are built by the way people communicate virtually.

- Sophisticated use of technology—people are power users who know how to make powerful human connections virtually.

- Fast, highly interactive human collaboration that is constantly going on virtually.

- Face-to-face travel is dramatically reduced because people are comfortable connecting virtually.

- Well orchestrated communication plan that preserves and builds team rapport around the world.

- eLeaders using technology to create a strong and visible leadership presence, from afar.

- Constant high-level interaction at multiple levels when people collaborate online (with Web conference technology, eTeamroom technology, and other collaborative tools)

Prepare People for HyperSpeed

3

> The first phase of the Internet was all about the browser, Web sites, and electronic mail. The second phase will be about even more deeply helping people connect with one another, [enhancing] communication between people and businesses in the richest and strongest of ways.
> **Steve Ballmer**
> **President and CEO**
> Microsoft

I n his thought-provoking book titled *Visions,* Harvard and Berkeley educated physicist Michio Kaku states that we have ended the Age of Discovery and entered the Age of Mastery.

Just reflect on that for a moment. For all of us, the 1990s was a decade of discovering the power, access, and fun of technology. Armed with our cell phones, pagers, and portable computers, we learned that we could be anywhere and still get connected—at least on a technical level. Sometimes we discovered technology's awesome power, and other times we discovered its many limitations. Unfortunately, many of those limitations had a human impact that we didn't discover until it was too late.

> No matter how much we tried to communicate, we discovered big holes in our communication, which drove big holes into trust, rapport, and sense of team.

We also discovered how to get connected to people from anywhere on the globe. We learned a lot about working across cultures, languages, and locations. We experimented with working from homes, cars, and other distant locations. We learned that we could work with other employees in our company located all over the world. Others expanded their long-distance teamwork to include people outside formal company boundaries: suppliers, partners, contractors, professional services, and even customers. We discovered the benefits of the frequent flyer programs and the shortcomings of spending too many hours in travel. Most discovered that their workload became much heavier, and balancing the needs of work with family was a major challenge.

> To be fast enough, eLeaders and eTeams are becoming intentionally smarter—not just about technology, but also how to use technology to build teamwork—fast—without travel.

In the Age of Discovery, we experimented with technology, tried to use it in different ways, and generally accepted its shortcomings. We created entities we called virtual teams, and by the end of the decade seven out of ten of us had worked on one. We barraged each other with e-mail, voice mail, and other digital communication in an effort to stay in touch. In fact, a study done by the Institute for the Future showed that business people had to handle over 200 pieces of communication a day—day after day.

No matter how much we tried to communicate, though, we discovered big holes in our communication, which drove big holes into trust, rapport, and sense of team. We discovered that we had to travel regularly to beef up trust and build sense of team. We had the time and the budget. Those days are gone.

The new millennium marks the beginning of the Age of Mastery. *To be fast enough, eLeaders and eTeams are becoming intentionally smarter—not just about technology, but also how to use technology to build teamwork—fast—without travel.* Intentionally smarter is about wisdom—that wonderful insight that people have because they pay attention to the world around them. Wisdom is learned from successes, and from failures. Wisdom is learned from life.

Wisdom has made one fact about communication through technology painfully clear. The plug-and-play myth is dead! If you want your team to collaborate from afar, it will take much more than a license or a link to any Web collaboration technology. It will take more than logging on, pressing a button, or attaching files. Some technology salespeople would have us believe that we only need to sign up or log on, and voilá, instant teamwork. If you believe that, I have a bridge in Brooklyn I would like to sell you.

We're a lot smarter than that. As Barbara Mayron of Sun Microsystems says, "Some people think they can move a live meeting into an online meeting and carry on as if we were all there. It doesn't work that way." The technology is intuitive. How to get distant people to collaborate with it isn't.

> *Collaborative technology is intuitive. How to get distant people to collaborate with it isn't.*

What mistakes do people make in getting a team to collaborate across distance? There are a lot of them, but they all boil down to those that follow.

Ways NOT to Create Team Collaboration at HyperSpeed

- Cut travel budgets and say, "Just meet online."
- Install or license collaborative groupware and assume, by technology's very presence on the computer desktop, that people will be transformed magically.

- Assume that plugging in or logging on is all that humans need for successful, high-level, online collaboration.

- Assume that collaborative technology is so intuitive that no training on how humans are to use it to be more effective is needed.

- Assume that the level of collaboration people do today, from afar, is as good as it gets.

- And, the big one, the mother of all mistakes: Ignore any and all human factors in getting people to collaborate across distance.

If you use any of the previous methods, after about a month, when the new technology has lost its sizzle, people will stop using it. When they see that a technology fails to produce tangible value, fails to make their world better, or fails to deliver on the human side—they will revert to e-mail and conference calls. What a tragedy!

> *Relationships and teamwork are critical for every team. Just plugging in isn't teamwork.*

We have the wisdom to know that the greatest challenge is for people to master how to use technology in ways that make a significant difference in team collaboration, decision making, and results. People want to know how to create warmth, trust, and sense of team from afar, and pressing buttons doesn't do that. Relationships and teamwork are critical for every team. Just plugging in isn't teamwork.

How to Lay the Right Foundation for HyperSpeed

Technology is sold in our world with great promises. It will make us faster, more productive, and more connected. It will enable a giant leap in performance for our people, our teams, and our company's bottom line. To realize the promise, you need the right approach.

Without a technology plan and training, eTeams get stuck in the Disabled and Mechanical Phases. To become Bionic, use a formula for success that works. The solution rests mostly in how we prepare our eTeams to use technology in human ways: to collaborate, connect, and interact at great speed, from afar.

The right way to get people to collaborate with technology is based on a study conducted by Drs. Christine V. Bullen and John L. Bennett. Their study, *Groupware in Practice: An Interpretation of Work Experience* (CISR WP No. 205), published through the Sloan School of Management's Center for Information Systems Research at the Massachusetts Institute of Technology, helps leaders see why some teams accelerate the process of acceptance and use of technology in human organizations. The study examined people and technology integration in 25 different industries.

What did Bullen and Bennett discover that made some groups employ software tools productively versus others that found no benefit? Their research confirmed that getting people to use technology—and use it effectively—is a human process. In fact, their study found four human factors made a significant difference. All four are critical for success.

1. *Champions.* Influential leadership supports the technology.

2. *Expectations.* The technology will be used to improve communication.

3. *Training.* Train people only on the features they will use right away.

4. *Evolution.* Provide continual training or resources to upgrade skills.

Let's take a look at each of these factors in more detail, linking their findings with the best practices of the Bionic eTeams you will meet in this book.

Collaboration through Technology Needs a Champion

A champion is a person who steps forward to inspire the team or organization to use a given technology. The champion has insight about the communication challenge that people in a virtual environment face. The champion has a clear picture of the level of teamwork that is required for success. Then the champion selects, finds, or charges the team to find the technology that enables the team to surmount the challenge it faces.

Champions are not people who buy technology for technology's sake. They aren't the ones who go out and buy a new technology just to be one of the first to have it. The champion may love her gadgets or technologies and often be at the cutting edge in using them. The single factor that makes someone a champion, however, is looking way beyond technology. A champion sees how a group works better, faster, and stronger as a team with technology—and without colocation.

> *A champion is looking way beyond technology to see a group that works better, faster, and stronger with technology.*

The champion can be anyone, anywhere in the organization. For large efforts to increase collaboration through technology, the champion can be high in the organization. He can be the CEO, president, corporate officer, or general manager. At that level, the champion can steer important resources and drive the eCollaboration initiative throughout the organization. In fact, they must lead the way by visibly improving their own ability to collaborate from afar themselves.

Champions can be at many other levels, as well. A team leader can champion a collaborative technology to improve team results. He can generate teamwork by using a selected technology to dramatically improve team interaction, meetings, and results. She can keep people focused on continually improving their effectiveness in collaborating without travel.

The champion can also be anyone on the team who knows technology well enough to help the group embrace its power.

In fact, people don't have to be on any formal team at all to be champions. All of us need to collaborate with people outside of any definition of team. Therefore, individuals can be their own champions in using technology in creative, effective ways.

Clearly, the champion has to understand how to use technology in ways that enable the group to simplify its work, collaborate better across distance, save time, and produce results, fast. Every technology integration will encounter turbulence, such as people getting dropped off a Web link. The champion needs to keep people positive and focused through that early transition period.

Champions also need to stay the course until the transition is complete. They need to give technology a purpose for being, a reason for people to use it. They also must make sure that best practices for collaborating on technology are shared globally, so everyone benefits every time it's used.

Set Clear Expectations, with a Human Face

The technology champion must set clear expectations for how the technology is to be used to improve teamwork. It is not enough to say, "Use Web conference technology for all meetings." Vague, general expectations will only produce vague, general results. People will log on to eMeetings or use the technology for show-and-tell presentations. When people see that the impact of using Web conference technology is negligible to none, they will stop logging on or stop attending the meeting.

> *Expectations with a human face take the focus away from technology and put it on people, teamwork, and human collaboration.*

Contrast that to a technology expectation with a human face: "Use Web conference technology in ways that enhance relationships with our customers." Now people have something tangible to attain that they can get excited about. Expectations with a human face take the focus away from technology and put it on people, teamwork, and human collaboration. The human focus stops people from thinking about what button to press on the software. Instead, they focus on how to use the software to engage customers in a warm and personal way.

Expectations should be even further clarified, in human terms. Leave no ambiguity in the human environment you are trying to create. Spell out expectations in writing, have them printed and mounted on a small reference card, and give it to each person to post on her computer monitor, in view during Web conferences.

Each eCollaboration technology that you use must have similar expectations set, written down, and at hand.

Train People Only on Human Methods and the Essential Technology Features People Will Use Now

You know the expression: Use it or lose it. It's good advice when training people to eCollaborate at HyperSpeed. Give people only as much as they can apply right now, today. Then stop. Let people digest what they have learned, practice it in their real work, and get comfortable with it. Only then should they be exposed to another set of best practices and technology features.

> Even though people use technology, the focus must be on communication, collaboration, and trust.

The wrong approach is to teach people only the basic, mechanical skills of how to operate the software. That kind of learning lasts only a few minutes after people leave the session. More importantly, the focus is on the wrong thing: technology—not communication, performance, rapport, or results.

Even though people use technology, the focus must be on communication, collaboration, and trust. Cover it one step at a time, and make sure that people use the methods right away. Provide support for those that need it, reinforcing that these are the new basic skills the team needs to collaborate effectively online.

Evolve People to Bionic eTeamwork Competence

Bullen and Bennett say that people reach a "plateau of competence" with technology. We get comfortable using the same software and features over and over again, and we get stuck there. We don't want to move on because we are comfortable. Besides, dealing with technology can be painful (especially when it doesn't work).

To create Bionic eTeamwork, our best practices and skills have to keep evolving. Therefore, people need more learning and support, one step at a time, in a fashion similar to the previous point. Technology will keep on evolving. If we don't continuously evolve our ability to use it, we get farther and farther behind.

> *If we are doing our work the same way we did it two years ago, one year ago, even six months ago—we are not evolving. Technology is.*

We can evolve with more training. We can use specialists, or as groups we can create our own training. The important part is the word *evolve.* If we are doing our work the same way we did it two years ago, one year ago, even six months ago—we are not evolving. Technology is. The market is. Your competition is. Don't be left in their exhaust fumes!

Some Final Thoughts . . .

Bionic eTeamwork requires technology leadership. It requires training that is more comprehensive and relevant than what buttons to press. Most technologies today are fairly intuitive. The magic occurs only when people learn how to use electronic tools to enhance their human ability to communicate— to build trust, to collaborate, to get results, and otherwise be more effective.

If teams don't find value in a tool, they'll stop using it. Teams used to be able to leave it and go back to old methods. Today, such a passive approach is deadly. Bionic eTeams seek out new technology to enable fast collaboration, then use this four-part plan to ensure that technology makes a difference in team collaboration and results.

Importantly, technology by itself doesn't create eTeamwork, but eTeamwork can be dramatically enhanced by the way a team uses technology to collaborate.

The key to making your eTeam fast and cohesive is how your team uses technology. It includes improving how you use current technologies, how you select new technologies, and how you integrate technology into making your team dramatically better. The work that eTeams do today is too fast and too complex for conference calls and e-mail alone. Although important technologies, they are too slow and filter out too many communication cues without help.

> *To become Bionic, eTeams must embrace collaborative technology, then introduce it in ways that drive high-performance teamwork.*

To become Bionic, eTeams must embrace collaborative technology, then introduce it in ways that drive high-performance teamwork. When done correctly, the payoffs are immense. The investment will pay back with interest for decades, because the team has a technology culture that is high functioning, well practiced, and knowledgeable about how to create results virtually.

B I O N I C

eTeamwork Checklist

Preparing People for HyperSpeed

This chapter began with a quote by Steve Ballmer, CEO of Microsoft, who said, *"The first phase of the Internet was all about the browser, Web sites, and electronic mail. The second phase will be about even more deeply helping people connect with one another, [enhancing] communication between people and businesses in the richest and strongest of ways."*

The Bionic eLeader's role is to help the team evolve out of the Disabled and Mechanical Phases and into the Bionic Phase. That means breaking old habits and ineffective, out-of-date practices. It also means building expertise in new, technologically-savvy best practices and technology.

Bionic eTeams are power users of technology. Power users seek technology that enables them to collaborate faster. Then they become highly skilled in how to use it to speed decisions, interaction, and results. "Almost as good as" or "as good as" traditional, face-to-face meetings are not good enough or fast enough. Bionic eTeams look for the quantum leap, then select the technology and training that is required for success.

To prepare your eTeam for HyperSpeed with technology, commit to a plan in writing to increase eCommunication expertise through technology. The plan has four critical success factors:

☐ *Designate a technology champion.* The champion commits to advocating the purchase of any needed software, supporting any needed training, and providing the leadership communication to create Bionic eCommunication. If you can't identify a leader higher in the organization, take on this personal responsibility yourself.

❒ *Set clear expectations, with a human focus.* It is not enough to say, "Use PlaceWare (a Web conference tool) for all eMeetings." Instead, "Use PlaceWare in ways that speed our decision making and buy-in."

❒ *Provide best-practice training, with the emphasis on communication, trust, and collaboration—not technology.* Make sure the training covers real-world simulations. Take a just-in-time approach, focused on human collaboration and teamwork, not technology.

❒ *Evolve skills across time.* Collaborating virtually requires a whole new world of communication expertise that can't be learned in one session or one day. This skill set is the most significant change in communication since people learned to speak. To collaborate at HyperSpeed, people's human eCollaboration expertise and best practices need continual upgrading.

THINGS YOU CAN DO TODAY TO
Prepare Your eTeam for HyperSpeed

eLeaders	eTeams	Individuals
HyperSpeed doesn't occur naturally. You have to provide leadership.	Get organized as a team to operate at HyperSpeed.	Get prepared as an individual to communicate at HyperSpeed.

eLeaders

HyperSpeed doesn't occur naturally. You have to provide leadership.

- Be the champion or find a champion to spearhead an eCollaboration culture.
- Select one critical technology at a time. Then set an expectation of how people are to use it to improve results and teamwork.
- Provide training focused on the *human* side of using that technology to create cohesive, fast eTeamwork.
- Keep advancing by sharing best practices and techniques, or get more training.

eTeams

Get organized as a team to operate at HyperSpeed.

- Identify eCommunication bottlenecks that break down results and eTeamwork.
- Identify critical eTeam technologies and the role each will play in teamwork.
- Get training in how to be power users of technology in ways that build teamwork and results.
- Create a clear and specific written eCommunication plan for that technology.

Individuals

Get prepared as an individual to communicate at HyperSpeed.

- Identify the technologies that help you collaborate across distance, particularly Web conferencing.
- Upgrade your human skills in using technology to create high-level collaboration, virtually.
- If your company does not directly provide a learning program, take responsibility for creating your own.

Getting InTouch

When to Travel

4

> *Technology won't make people interact. It only gives them a forum to do that. If you want people to use technology to collaborate, let them get to know each other first.*
>
> **Maridan A. Clements**
> Philips Components eBusiness

The team of 18 arrived on time for the 7 AM meeting. While the leader went over the agenda for the three-day session, I looked around the room. Have you ever looked into eyes that are looking at the leader, yet appear lifeless—almost zombielike?

Now some of you might be saying to yourself that at 7 AM everyone's eyes look that way! This team's eyes were infinitely more so. Five members of this team had flown from Moscow to Texas, arriving the previous evening. The other 13 members, however, were all from Texas—in fact, from the very city where the team was meeting. Yet their eyes, too, reflected that same emptiness.

Shortly after the leader's introductory remarks, the leader's pager went off. The next thing we knew, he had left the room for the rest of the day. The following day he spent only two hours with the team. On the third day, he stayed almost the whole day, but his preoccupation with the files he brought with him showed that he wasn't mentally there.

The agenda was filled with three full days of team alignment, project management, and a few team building activities. The leader had scheduled no social outings, except one dinner out the first night. All of the lunches were half-hour working lunches, so people could save time for all of the other meetings they had to attend outside of the workshop. The focus was clearly on work and on maximizing the number of business issues this team could complete while they were all in the same location.

There was no spark in this team, no momentum, and no life. The leader was clearly out of touch with the people, and the human needs, of this team. As a result, the team was equally as out of touch. This was not a *dis*connected team; it was *un*connected. It is an example of a severe failure in eLeadership.

Strive to Create InTouch

Every Bionic eTeam knows that relationships are too important to be left to chance. They have worked on enough effective and ineffective virtual teams to know that teamwork is about people, not technology. The relationships and connections that people build are reflected in the collaboration that occurs when people are apart. If you want people to collaborate from afar, let them travel first.

Bionic eTeams are in a constant quest, therefore, to create high-trust relationships and a vibrant sense of team. They want to experience both when people are together, and especially when they are apart. They believe that a team whose spirit is alive and well will outperform one that has no spirit or whose spirit is dying.

Although some virtual teams perform well without any travel, they are quite unusual. No matter how much technology the team has or uses, people are human. Shaking each other's hand, breaking bread over dinner, laughing while playing baseball together—these human moments connect us, inspire us, and boost team relationships faster than any other method.

Every team struggles to ignite its spark and unleash the talent it pulls together from all over the world. Few achieve spark without travel. Virtual teamwork works best when people meet each other first.

Therefore, Bionic eTeams approach onsite meetings with an overriding singular purpose: to create InTouch.

InTouch is a human connection Bionic eTeams intentionally build, linking people to each other and invoking the joy of working together on a human level. InTouch is the heart and soul of Bionic eTeamwork.

InTouch goes beyond "high tech, high touch," which implies that humanity needs to be a part of the high-tech workplace. Instead, *InTouch means a strong human connection purposefully created through communication.* InTouch is an essential element of eTeam success.

> *Although some virtual teams perform well without any travel, they are quite unusual.*

Getting InTouch is not something that people on eTeams do when they have time. No, quite the contrary. High-trust relationships are mandatory for inspired levels of success. As such, being InTouch is a forethought, never an afterthought. It's a major part of the eTeam's day and actions. Being InTouch pays off big, both in the heart and on the bottom line.

InTouch isn't only about having the team travel to one place to have dinner together, play softball together, or have some experience together. Although these informal opportunities to be together are important, they are not enough. Many teams travel to be together in one place, have a great time, and continue their Mechanical or Disabled teamwork upon return to their dispersed locations.

> *InTouch is about intent to connect and effort to create trusting relationships.*

> **Bionic eTeams approach trust directly, with vigor.**

Instead, InTouch is about *intent* to connect and *effort* to create trusting relationships. For eTeams, InTouch focuses on how to build relationships, increase rapport, and work better as a team. It is about building excitement and unity around the work, the way the team will work together, and the human value of why the work is important.

Bionic eTeams *never* take a passive approach about trust or relationships. Rather, they approach each directly, with vigor, actively designing their interaction to lay a positive foundation to positive human relationships and results.

Travel to Build Relationships, Not Do the Work

To create Bionic eTeamwork, travel isn't an expense. It's an investment in team collaboration, from afar.

People collaborate best with people that they feel they know and/or are comfortable with. Even in this high-technology business environment, face-to-face visits are still the most comfortable way for people to establish rapport.

> **Technology doesn't eliminate the need for travel.**

The key differentiator about travel, however, is not just that people get together in one place. Travel is a given— a necessary step for all teams that work from separate sites. Instead, the key factor that creates Bionic eTeamwork focuses on what people do when they travel. *For Bionic eTeamwork, people travel to create rapport more than to do the work.*

In the Disabled and Mechanical Phases of teamwork, people feel they have to travel to interact, collaborate, and communicate effectively about the work. Buried in one room together, they plaster the walls with flip chart notes. They consume the day sitting through endless slide presentations and volumes of handouts. Because the presentations go on too long, the team runs out of time. The first time people interact is in the van back to the airport. Everyone has all too little time to engage in enough conversation to create InTouch.

In the Bionic Phase, teams know they can collaborate faster, make decisions faster, and participate faster with Web conference, electronic teamroom, and other online collaborative technologies, from afar. Rather than relying on vague nonverbal cues in face-to-face meetings, they know they can use live polls to determine level of agreement and buy-in. Rather than listening to presentations in one room, they can participate in the presentations better through Web conference technology. Rather than carting back heavy paper files on the airplane, they know they can access the latest version in their electronic teamroom.

Teams that take the Bionic approach have more time to develop InTouch. They don't waste a single minute of rare face-to-face time on anything that they can cover from afar. *Travel to improve rapport, not do the work.*

Eliminate Distractions, and *Be There*

Being in the same physical space isn't the same as *being there*.

Being there means being mentally present, in the moment, with the people that are in each other's presence. *Being there* means giving our full attention to each other, communicating together in a way that is free of distractions from other sources. It is a focus on human communication and interaction at the moment, so that human rapport, trust, and sense of team flourish.

> *Travel to improve rapport, not do the work.*

Bionic eTeams work very hard to keep distractions from interrupting the very rare time when people are in one location. They know all too well the greatest pitfall to *being there* with each other: distractions. In the course of a year, hundreds of thousands of distractions hammer away, noisily trying to invade InTouch time and InTouch moments.

In fact, a study conducted by Pitney Bowes in conjunction with the Institute for the Future showed that in the Year 2000, people all over the world were deluged. The number of messages sent and received on a typical day per person in the United States is 204. Although the lion's share is e-mail, others include voice mail, telephones, pagers, cell phones, faxes, overnight courier/messages, Post-it notes, telephone message slips, postal mail, and interoffice mail. The study also showed similar high totals in other countries: the United Kingdom had 191; Germany, 176; France, 165; and Canada, 160.

> *The number of messages sent and received on a typical day per person in the United States is 204.*

In addition, the Pitney Bowes/Institute for the Future study shows another key distraction. People are working many projects and work on many teams in any given work week. In the United States, office workers are on 16.9 teams; the United Kingdom, 12.5; Canada. 13.6; Germany, 10.6; and France 9.5. The UK workers were on the most work teams: 9.1. Others included U.S. workers on 7.2 different teams; Canada on 5.4; France on 3.1; and Germany on 2.5 teams. Each team comes with its urgent moments and its unique demands on people's attention.

> *In the United States, office workers are on 16.9 teams.*

It's no wonder that so many virtual teams meet offsite. They have to pry themselves away from demands of the rest of the world so they can focus on *this* team's people, *this* team's trust, and *this* team's interaction. Bionic eTeams are very sensitive to choose "neutral" locations, such as hotels, not the normal business office. Isolation at an offsite location (versus the normal office) creates an environment for people to *be there* and create InTouch.

At offsites, most Bionic eTeams also choose to turn off all cell phones and pagers. Others designate only a few times during the day for outside communication. Of course, the world doesn't stop because a team is having an offsite meeting. So, in the case of emergencies, Bionic eTeams have an emergency contact plan, in case a major emergency erupts that day (which it sometimes does).

People that travel to meet in one place have a choice in how to handle distractions. The way people handle that choice will always have a significant impact on the level of InTouch that they create when they are in that rare face-to-face communication environment.

Take one leader of an eTeam that worked 1,500 miles away from the others. After three months, the leader of the eTeam finally made a trip to the eTeam members' location in Florida for the first time. The closest airport was about a one-hour drive from the office

> *Being in the same physical space isn't the same as being there.*

where the three worked. One of the eTeam members, in an effort to try to establish a better relationship with the eLeader, offered to pick him up at the airport. The eTeam member felt the time would be well invested, because it would give him an extra two hours (one hour each way) of informal and private time to talk with the eLeader.

The leader's plane arrived. They walked to the eTeam member's car and got in. They engaged in small talk that started off well. About ten minutes out of the airport, the eLeader said, "I forgot my cell phone. I notice, though, that you have a car phone. Can I use it to make a call?" To be courteous, the eTeam member said yes. The one call the eLeader made was to check his voice mail. For the rest of the one-hour trip, he was consumed processing the stack of voice mail. He didn't hang up until the two of them pulled in the parking lot of their firm's office building. Being in the same physical space isn't the same as *being* there.

How would you feel if you were the eTeam member? He said he felt more like a chauffeur that had been taken advantage of. Instead of building the relationship, the interaction had damaged what little there was up to that point.

Contrast the previous example with this one. Another leader of an eTeam worked 500 miles from a team member. After about three months, the eLeader made a trip to Denver to visit the eTeam member for the first time. The eLeader flew in that morning and had to leave late that afternoon—allowing about seven hours on the ground in Denver.

Time was very limited. Denver's airport is about an hour's trip north of the city. If the eLeader rented a car and drove to the location, the two would only have about four hours. Wanting more time with the eLeader, the eTeam member offered to pick up and drop off the eLeader at the airport. He accepted.

> *In onsite visits, reach out to create a foundation for a trusting relationship.*

The two spent the entire day together. The eLeader, a vice president in the bank, focused his entire day on developing a relationship with the eTeam member. They spent the whole day in conversations that built a respectful, positive relationship. They talked about their interests, joys, and values; their families and lives; and other personal topics. They conversed about the work, the customers, the frustrations, and the joys.

> *InTouch will happen if people want it to happen and jointly take action to make it happen.*

They visited with some customers and created excellent rapport about their attitude toward finding and keeping customers. They came to agree on how to work well together and make customers happy. They had lively discussions about their families, interests, and life goals. Every minute of their time together, the two actively reached out to create a foundation for a trusting relationship. At the end of the day when they returned to the airport, they were connected.

In the Denver example, the eLeader was really *there,* as was the eTeam member. Neither let other distractions eat away their limited time to connect on a personal level. Neither put on a show for each other, but instead communicated in a genuine, respectful way. Both entered this onsite visit with *intent* and *effort.* The payoff was a solid foundation that both created together.

Getting InTouch is an active process. It is created with *intent* because people want to develop trust. It is created with *effort*—specifically, the behaviors and the communication that clearly demonstrate the desire to connect on a human level. It doesn't matter if people speak different languages, come from different countries and cultures, or work for different companies. InTouch will happen if people want it to happen and jointly take action to make it happen.

By choosing to eliminate distractions and focus on *being there,* people are better able to create InTouch.

Make It Comfortable for People to Connect with You

When teams travel to be at one site, InTouch is more than one person trying to get connected with another on the team. The latter must also want to connect with the former, as well. Relationships are reciprocal. They are built one at a time, and every relationship is unique. Relationships require constant care and constant vigil.

It doesn't matter whether you are a leader, a member of an eTeam, or a single individual who wants to create In-Touch with someone in an onsite visit. Relationships take time and attention.

> *Relationships give any group its life, its heart, and its soul.*

Relationships give any group its life, its heart, and its soul. When done well, relationships flourish from afar. They pay off not only in joy and teamwork, but also in dedication and results.

Many people struggle with how to create a personal connection with a virtual team of three or five or ten people. Imagine the formidable task of doing that with a virtual organization of 10,000. Under the leadership of Jimmy Treybig, former CEO of Tandem Computers, Tandem grew into a $10 billion powerhouse that was recognized as number one in service and regularly numbered among the 100 best companies.

What insights about InTouch does a CEO have that everyone can benefit from and use? Treybig was a master at making something that seems so formidable, so easy to understand and embrace. He said, "Communication is why we were in the top 100."

Now, many eLeaders say that communication is important. When we look at how eLeaders spend their time, however, it's clear that many only pay lip service to communication. In contrast, Treybig showed his commitment to communication daily in his actions and in the way he masterfully drove InTouch at Tandem.

> *Well-managed communication focuses on how to energize people as a team and how to create personal, human connections around the globe.*

Treybig said, "Communication has to be well managed." He wasn't talking about how to format e-mail messages. Instead, well-managed communication focuses on how to energize people as a team and how to create personal, human connections around the globe. InTouch was part of that plan.

To be more specific, Treybig had to create InTouch with him as the leader, and the people had to create InTouch with each other. The intent of that effort, according to Treybig, was that "when we got big, people were truly connected around the world."

As the CEO, he was not a leader that the company employees only read about in a company newspaper or Web site. Treybig was a presence that spanned the globe, not just through articles or e-mails about him, but from the personal way he connected and aligned his people for success. This presence was no accident. It was part of Treybig's plan to keep people InTouch—in a highly human way—with him, with each other, with corporate officers, with customers, and with the exciting direction and success Tandem created as a worldwide organization.

Human trust and connections are important, but they can be challenging to create when people aren't in the same place. "Creating trust is hard to do with e-mail," continued

Treybig, in his warm, hospitable, Texas manner. "We communicated heavily through technology. But you have to have the personal part, too, like the town meeting or the beer blast, so people will like me. Love, if I can use that word, then makes other communication effective. Leaders have to create trust and love to make all communication effective."

Few can dispute Treybig's words. People who have a positive connection with one another will receive a message very differently than people who have a strained one. Besides, as Treybig said, *"If you want a great company, people won't tell you what is wrong unless they trust you."* Therefore, creating positive InTouch connections with him and with each other was a critical part of Treybig's plan for success.

You may have noticed Treybig's use of the word *love.* How many times have you heard people use the word *love* in business? Maybe never? Some don't feel it. Some are afraid to feel it. And some feel it, but are hesitant to express it. Love is a word that clearly indicates how InTouch Treybig was with his company's people and the human side of his company's work. I found the interview energizing, genuine, and refreshing.

Bionic eTeamwork begins with our humanity—loving what we do, making our customers happy, and building our human network. Clearly these goals were drivers for this Bionic eLeader.

Include Partners, Customers in Your eTeam

Once, on a trip to Hawaii, I sat next to a person who was traveling from San Francisco to Japan for a one-hour business meeting. Most people won't travel anywhere for a one-hour meeting—especially an 18-hour trip across the Pacific Ocean. If the jet lag doesn't get you, the food will. But for the product development leader who was sitting next to me, the trip was essential. Working with the Japanese was new for his company. Relationships were so critical for success that one hour of face to face, followed by an evening of informal conversation, was an essential part of establishing rapport and trust.

The virtual workplace has opened some of the most exciting—and challenging—team environments that business professionals around the world have ever known. Picture a team that spans two very successful companies that are competitors in some markets and partners in another. Add to that the cultural differences of a team that spans the Pacific Ocean. One culture is from the United States; the other, Japan. Add on dramatically different languages that have no common alphabet and that frequently require interpreters for people to communicate.

Such was the challenge of the Hewlett Packard (HP) LaserJet-Canon Team. Largely because of their commitment to communicate and build a real team that spanned the Pacific Ocean, they surmounted that enormous challenge. Many independent sources consider this team one of the most successful strategic alliances in the industry.

> *Our relationship with Canon is a real partnership of professional and personal relationships built over the years. That is what makes it work.*

In this alliance, HP and Canon have worked successfully together for 15 years, an accomplishment in itself. Starting with one printer, their alliance now produces an array of top-quality products and consumables. HP Laser Printers holds an impressive 70 to 75 percent market share (higher in some markets, and lower in others) in an extremely competitive marketplace.

This team was masterful in the many ways that they created InTouch. Their intent and their actions clearly showed that human connections were at the forefront of their success strategy. In fact, a high-trust, high-respect relationship was so important that it was identified as a core competence for the people on the team.

One level of InTouch focused on the human alliance of the two companies. In this alliance, Hewlett Packard develops, manufactures, and markets the printers. Canon is the key supplier of most engines (the majority of mechanical parts inside the printers). The leadership team from Hewlett Packard is in Idaho, and the leadership team from Canon is in Japan.

Neal Martini, Senior Vice President and General Manager of LaserJet Business Printers, says, "Our relationship with Canon is not treated as a vendor-buyer relationship. Rather, it is a *real* partnership of professional and personal relationships built over the years. That is what makes it work."

Martini's point is key. In this age of global teams, the words *partnerships* and *alliances* have become common. Unlike the HP LaserJet-Canon Team, however, most aren't partnerships at all. In pseudopartnerships and pseudo-alliances, one company has the dollars and acts as the buyer.

> *Partnerships and alliances don't work if one loses.*

The other needs or does the work, and acts as the vendor. Their relationship is the result of a contract and has little to do with deep, trusting personal connections among the people. It also has little to do with teamwork, sense of team, and mutual win/win.

In contrast, real partnerships are obvious by the actions of the people. Once again, the HP LaserJet-Canon Team sets the standard. Reflecting the wisdom that no doubt elevated him to his important position, Martini contin-ues, "We look at our relationship as long term, not a one-time deal. As such, we genuinely try to make all deci-

> *Both joined forces to leverage their alliance to grow opportunities and revenues for both of their companies.*

sions a win/win. We work together to optimize our competitive position, optimize Canon's returns, and optimize ours. That is the only way our relationship can be successful. It doesn't work if one of us loses because of the relationship." Partnerships and alliances don't work if one loses.

The win/win, then, isn't just that HP buys product from Canon. It isn't just that when HP sells more printers, Canon makes revenues from making more printer parts. Real partner-ships are much more than that. The HP LaserJet-Canon Team partnership goes forward a critical step that truly differentiates lip service partners from real partners. *Both joined forces to leverage their alliance to grow opportunities and revenues for both of their companies.* This might involve collaborating to create more products, better products, and gain stronger market position.

Even though many of the original people have moved on, the relationships that were created and carefully built over the years have added to the cohesiveness of the team. Still, however, this team consciously spends time improving them.

Interact about How to Team Better

What do the entire teams meet about when they come together? Face-to-face time is treated as a unique time to energize the people, refocus the team, and learn how to become an even better team.

Both the HP LaserJet-Canon Team and CEO Treybig's team of 10,000 at Tandem had creative, effective ways to build sense of team and real teamwork when people traveled.

Once a year, for example, the HP LaserJet-Canon Team holds a "Dream Team" meeting. For so many virtual teams, when people travel to be in one location, much of that time is spent on business issues. The focus is on making sure everyone understands the charter, the work, or the changes. Martini's team did not get caught in that "task only" trap.

Martini said, "Our Dream Team meeting is not structured to talk about tactical issues. Rather, it is about visioning. It focuses on how we and our people will work together." Of course, they had other meetings to talk about tactical issues. Martini's Dream Team meeting, however, was dedicated solely to improve InTouch.

Tandem Computers had a similar approach to onsite meetings, only Tandem's weren't called Dream Team meetings. Instead, they were called TOPs—Tandem Outstanding People.

In line with Treybig's InTouch focus, the purpose of TOPs was to promote togetherness, understanding, and respect across all of Tandem's locations around the world. Four times a year, 250 of Tandem's best people were awarded the honor of participating in TOPs.

Every employee in every job in every location around the world was eligible for TOPs. Some people attended more than once over the years. At each TOPs session, people traveled to be in one location. For one week, the whole group immersed itself in the exciting challenge of how to build a great company.

> *A leader's intent to have people like him or her is not about stroking that person's ego.*

If you have ever tried to get on a CEO's schedule, you know how difficult it is. Every minute of the executive's day is committed to someone, some group, or some cause. Time is finite, and demand for an executive's time always exceeds availability. Thus, how an executive spends time reflects his true priorities. When it came to TOPs, Treybig attended every one. He made it a point to meet and talk with every person. He learned their names and established a positive connection with each. The purpose of TOPs was to get InTouch—connected not only with him and each other, but also the strategy, the philosophy, and the joy of creating a great company. Treybig gladly invested four weeks of his calendar at TOPs, because InTouch was a critical part of the foundation the company needed for global success.

Bionic eLeaders are very open about the importance and value of creating trust. Treybig felt that it was important to be InTouch with as many of his people as he could. He said, "When you lead 10,000 people, how many can know me? Not very many. But if every site has four or five people that speak highly of me, then that lays the foundation for everyone else."

> *Leaders, individual team members, or individuals may need to travel alone, on occasion.*

People work harder for someone they like than for someone they don't. So, a leader's intent to have people like him or her is not about stroking that person's ego. Rather, it is about creating InTouch connections—a critical component to ensure Bionic eTeamwork.

This same InTouch foundation paid off among the TOPs participants, too. Treybig added, "I can still visualize a secretary in Singapore interacting with a person from France. TOPs enabled personal links among our very best people. It provides a foundation of extreme loyalty and self-management."

Beginning with Treybig's focus on InTouch, Tandem created a uniquely successful "way of life" that still warms the hearts of the people that were a part of this amazing corporate culture. Treybig's leadership on so many levels was well ahead of its time—and clearly Bionic.

Go Offsite to Make Onsite Visits

All onsite visits won't be with the team. Leaders, individual team members, or individuals may need to travel alone, on occasion as well. People who take the time to travel make a very powerful nonverbal statement. Among many others, an in-person visit says to the people at that location . . .

- You are important. I have just invested my time in travel to be with you.
- Your office is important. I validate that the people at your office make an important contribution to our success.
- Your work is important. I validate that the people at this location do good work that adds value.
- I care that you feel included. Your participation is important on this team.
- I care that you are happy. I am here to see how I can help and support you so that you are satisfied.

Let's meet another notable Bionic eLeader who was masterful in creating InTouch. One of the most successful businessmen in America was Sam Walton, founder of Wal-Mart. He knew the value of human connections.

From the beginning, Walton made a point of visiting every Wal-Mart store at every opportunity. When he had only two stores in Arkansas, making a personal visit was easy. When his stores numbered over 1,200, he still met that commitment. Amazingly, every year he made a personal visit to every store!

Certainly, as a leader of such a successful company, Walton could have stayed in his office and had everyone come to see him. He could have had people generate endless reports that he could view at his desk. He could have sent out other people to do the work for h im as the company became huge. But that was not Walton's nature. It also was not part of his personal plan for success. Walton wanted to see his people, know his people, and thank his people—in person. He wanted to be InTouch.

When a leader visits a "remote" location, that visit is one of the most powerful ways a leader says, "You are important to me." An onsite visit honors people, validates their work, and underscores their importance as part of a global organization. Onsite visits were not something Walton scheduled when he had time. He made time for them, because the onsite visit conveyed a message well beyond words. When Walton was onsite, he created InTouch with Wal-Mart employees. He wasn't quickly shuttled past the employees to spend the bulk of his time in the store manager's office. Quite the contrary. He was there for his people. He was there to be and talk with all of them.

> *When a leader visits a "remote" location, that visit is one of the most powerful ways a leader says, "You are important to me."*

When Walton died, he was the richest man in America. Wal-Mart had become the largest retail store, overtaking Sears and K-Mart. In only 29 years, he transformed his first Wal-Mart store into a retailing empire that ranked number 4 on the Fortune 100 list, just below GM, Ford, and Exxon.

Some eLeaders think their job is only about finance. Walton saw his job as leadership—inspiring people, honoring the work, and creating joy and alignment toward the future. His actions show consistent intent and overwhelming effort to create InTouch with the people in his worldwide organization. Once the human connection is made among the people and humanity of the work, the financials will follow.

A Few Final Words

No matter how much technology surrounds it, Bionic eTeamwork always focuses first on its humanity—its mandate to create trust, rapport, and momentum. When people eagerly invest their time and resources to create InTouch, the payoffs are commensurate. InTouch is created fastest with a face-to-face visit up front. Many teams hold these events offsite, so the team can focus on creating InTouch, without distraction.

These Bionic eTeam leaders, however, know that their success is built first on human relationships. They know how easy it is to forget to attend to relationships when virtual—you know, the out of sight, out of mind thing. They know how easy it is to rely on the person who works right outside the door, to the exclusion of people that work elsewhere, want to contribute, and want to make a difference.

> Getting InTouch is about cohesion—getting the human part to gel.

None of these Bionic eLeaders let distance or technology be an excuse for weak relationships. Trusting personal relationships across all locations was fundamental to their success.

You didn't see a lot in this chapter about specific technology or about "fast" yet. Bionic eTeamwork always begins first with human connections. Getting InTouch is about cohesion—getting the human part to gel. This chapter is more like filling your Porsche or BMW with gas before you put the pedal to the metal on the highway. As one of the leaders said, "Sometimes you have to go slow to go fast."

BIONIC
eTeamwork Checklist

Create InTouch: When to Travel

This chapter began with this quote: "Technology won't make people interact. It only gives them a forum to do that. If you want people to use technology to collaborate, let them get to know each other first."

The Bionic eLeader's role is to help the team get InTouch with each other on a human level.

No matter how much technology surrounds an eTeam, teamwork is first and foremost a human process. People have to create trust and a sense of connection so they work well together. *The fastest way to give trust a boost is through strategic travel with the primary focus of accelerating human relationships.*

The foundation for high performance eTeamwork isn't your e-mail system. It's the trust and rapport your people build. Even though travel takes time and budget, all of the very successful eLeaders interviewed for this book (including all of them not featured in this chapter) saw *some* travel as a key investment in boosting sense of team and results. If your team has to collaborate well across distance, traditional face-to-face communication offers the most powerful environment to boost human trust up front.

To create InTouch, Bionic eLeaders and eTeams do these things:

☐ Strive to create InTouch.

☐ Travel to build relationships, not do the work.

☐ Eliminate distractions, and *be there.*

☐ Make it comfortable for people to connect with you.

☐ Take extra special care with international eTeams.

☐ Interact about how to team better.

☐ Go offsite to make onsite visits.

THINGS YOU CAN DO TODAY TO
Build InTouch in Onsite Visits

eLeaders	eTeams	Individuals
It is important that people like you and bond with you and each other. Create a plan to build InTouch in any form of onsite visit. *In onsite meetings, make fostering relationships at least as important as any technical or business purposes.* Build relationships: • With you as the eLeader. • Within your eTeam. • With any distant person that you must collaborate with or depend on.	It is important that people on the eTeam like each other and bond on a human level. • Negotiate the travel you need to boost relationships within the team. • Hold a Dream Team meeting focused on relationships, specifically how people can work better together, when apart. • While people are together at one site, have social events that build relationships *across* locations.	Travel is sometimes, but not always, required or needed to create the relationships needed for effective one-to-one collaboration. • If you must collaborate at very high and very interactive levels with one specific person, traveling to boost the relationship is usually a wise investment. • Routine, lower-level collaboration with many different individuals will not require travel.

5

Building InTouch, Virtually

> *I like the freedom of being remote. But I can't stand being ignored.*
> **Bob Smith, Manufacturing Manager**
> A Medical Manufacturing Company

Tom was the sales manager for a major book company. During his seven-year tenure, sales steadily grew at a healthy rate. Things were going well, and he was happy in his work.

One day, his assistant walked into his office and said, "Tom, this fax just came in. You need to read it now." Reluctantly, Tom dropped what he was doing and read it, stunned. The company had been bought out by another. The fax gave high-level information about the acquisition. It said that more information would be forthcoming. There had been no warning. Of course, he wondered about his job. When he reflected on his impressive sales figures, though, he thought his job was safe.

Two hours later, his assistant came in with another fax and said, "Tom, another fax came in. You had better sit down before you read it." Tom didn't even notice that his jaw dropped as the words stung his heart. He was terminated—by fax!

> *Most virtual teams spend 99 percent of their time apart.*

For two days, he tried calling his boss (who worked 900 miles away) to find out if there was some mistake. When he could only reach his boss's voice mail, he also called some other executives at headquarters. Every call went to voice mail. Even though every executive had an assistant, no one answered the phones live. When he called his peers, however, he found that he wasn't alone. Two others had received the same ice-cold fax, while others were spared that bombshell.

One of Tom's peers that survived the icy, vicious, virtual downsizing said, "Before this happened, I gave this company 200 percent of my energy, time, and passion. After this treatment by upper management of my friends, I'll just work my 8 to 5 job. I will never look at my work or my company in the same way again." In two years, she quit, too.

Building InTouch, Virtually

> *Don't wait for the face-to-face visit to build trust, rapport, and camaraderie. Create InTouch every time you communicate from afar.*

Traveling to create InTouch is the fastest way to give relationships a boost. It is not, however, the only way that teams create InTouch. In fact, most virtual teams spend 99 percent of their time apart. Therefore, it is even more important that every eTeam create a specific plan to ensure that InTouch is created and grows, from afar. In other words, don't wait for the face to face visit to build trust, rapport, and camaraderie. Create InTouch every time you communicate from afar.

People that have the intent and make the effort to build InTouch can create trust and rapport in any environment—face-to-face or virtual. Take Amy Lauder, Marketing Manager for a small consulting firm. Amy has a sparkle in her voice and a respect in her words that create instant InTouch by phone, which is how she made most of her contacts with her customers.

In one of her marketing campaigns, she sent Starbucks certificates, along with a one-page invitation to "share a cup of Joe" with her, virtually. Nearly everyone that she contacted responded, and people remembered her by name. Throughout the year that she held her job, people consistently called her back and stayed in touch. She had the intent and made the effort to create InTouch, virtually. It worked.

InTouch can be created—or destroyed—by the way people communicate virtually. Can people that have never met face to face build InTouch, from afar? Yes, they can, if they focus on creating InTouch when they communicate from afar. A face-to-face visit up front typically gives InTouch a boost, enabling people to build trust faster and deeper.

Building InTouch virtually, however, is a very slippery slope. If you have ever gone sledding on a really steep hill, you know how difficult it is to walk up the incline. If you've ever tried it, you also know how fast and easy it is to slip, then slide all the way to the bottom. Sometimes you might get halfway up the hill, suddenly lose your footing,

> *InTouch can be created—or destroyed—by the way people communicate virtually.*

and find yourself careening to the bottom. You have to tread the hill carefully, just as eTeams must tread eCommunication carefully, so that trust is built, not lost.

Take Maria and Ellen. Both worked on the same project together and exchanged many e-mails. InTouch was progressing well. Then Maria forgot to tell Ellen that she was going on vacation for a week. She also didn't know how to set Outlook so that it would automatically generate an "I'm on vacation" e-mail in her absence. When Maria returned, she had a host of progressively negative e-mails from Ellen because Maria had not responded to her requests.

InTouch is about trust, rapport, and goodwill. When people are apart, InTouch can blow up from a single mistake. In the example, Maria forgot to tell Ellen she would be on vacation. The greatest problem is that the offender may not even know there is a problem. Maria was happily on vacation and had no clue until she returned and read the e-mails. From her distant location (vacation), she couldn't see the problem until it was huge.

Trust can be broken intentionally, as it was for Tom in the termination-by-fax story that opened this chapter. As Tom said, 'When you have had great performance reviews, great numbers, and have embraced your job eagerly, the least that the company can do is have someone deliver that kind of news face to face."

You can make your best guess whether his boss and the other executives were intentionally not available. The fax was clearly the wrong medium for the message. It created a trust-breaking explosion that was felt by every employee around the world.

> *Communication that builds InTouch is too important to be left to chance.*

Trust can also be broken unintentionally through virtual communication. Take one eLeader who scheduled a video conference (VC) meeting. She booked the VC meeting room in her building for all of the people who were at her site, plus she booked one in the Chicago office for her Chicago team member. She sent the invitations two weeks in advance. On the day of the meeting, the Chicago team member went to the appointed room. After 20 minutes, no one showed up. After making some calls, it was only then that the Chicago team member discovered that the meeting had been rescheduled—and had taken place the previous day. No one thought to tell her about the change.

The eLeader did not intentionally exclude the Chicago team member. However, this kind of forgetfulness was a regular problem, as was failing to send handouts and slides during eMeetings. Each time people "just forgot," team InTouch was eroded. The people at the distant sites never made a big scene about it. In fact, only one of them brought it up verbally, once. However, each time it happened, the distant team members felt less and less connection to the team.

Communication that builds InTouch is too important to be left to chance.

Because trust can be broken so quickly—often in ways that will never be perceived at other locations—Bionic eLeaders, eTeams, and individuals create an eCommunication plan. The sole focus of the plan is to create, preserve, and build InTouch when people are not physically in one location.

Every Bionic eLeader who was interviewed for this book had a plan to build InTouch when the people on the eTeam were in a virtual environment. Each one, however, had a unique approach. This chapter gives you some ideas to help you shape your approach.

Use Collaborative Technology in Ways That Build Relationships

How do teams build rapport when people are not in one place? Many think that the only way we can develop rapport is to travel to be in one location. That is no longer true. New collaborative technology is opening exciting, powerful ways for people to create InTouch with significantly less travel.

Take Wendy Johnson, Account Manager at Chute Gerdeman, a full-service retail design firm that serves some of the best-known retailers, manufacturers, and service providers worldwide. Some of those clients include Red Lobster, Sara Lee, Stride Rite, Eddie Bauer, and CompUSA. Chute Gerdeman's sole purpose is to help clients increase sales and create brand buzz.

> *New collaborative technology is opening exciting, powerful ways for people to create InTouch with significantly less travel.*

Johnson said, "For years, Chute Gerdeman relied on its 'War Rooms' to work closely with our clients, project team members, and members of their extended team." War Rooms were physical rooms in their office where teams would interact on campaigns. Many people had to travel to meet in the War Room. In between travel, team members stayed in touch with e-mail, FedEx, and conference calls. In slower times, the physical War Room concept worked well.

Then the Internet economy boomed. Suddenly, the War Room was too slow. So, Chute Gerdeman took a major leap. They transformed their physical War Room into customized, digital War eRooms, one for each client. They used an internet-based technology, Instinctive's eRoom <www.eroom .com>, which let Chute Gerdeman establish a password-protected online space. Each client could see, annotate, and manage the myriad of documents, campaigns, and other team files that was this team's work.

The way the team at Chute Gerdeman, including its customers, used the technology was Bionic. They designed the eRoom to evolve the relationship with the client—and the team itself—to a whole new level. The War eRoom enabled everyone on the team to collaborate faster, manage review cycles better, and keep projects on track. These changes are notable, by themselves. But there's more.

Johnson said that with the War eRoom, "We created better communication and more interaction with the client throughout the project. We don't save six weeks' worth of work waiting for the next plane trip. Instead, we interact with our client and each other nearly every day through eRoom." The entire team used the War eRoom to exchange a steady flow of work daily, get client feedback on it, and make modifications right away. The result: better communication and better InTouch.

Johnson's greatest surprise was how it improved InTouch with the customer. She said, "We were able to improve our relationships with our customer—the most important person on our team. Chute Gerdeman is a fee-based company. The way the entire team interacted through eRoom shows respect by saving our client money, saving our client time, and giving our client choices that build our relationship."

She continued, "Every project that we do for a client has a dedicated budget. If we can cut travel time, we have more hours to build a better solution for the client, which builds the relationship. If the client wants us to travel, we can do that, too, which builds the relationship. We honor their need for economy, speed, or travel, which builds the relationship."

The important point is that the way people used eRoom technology enhanced InTouch. They used eRoom to facilitate communication and collaboration from anywhere, anytime. They simplified collaboration by its easy posting and tracking of documents. They called each other up on the phone to discuss or interact about certain files. They communicated more often with less stress, which resulted in greater InTouch.

Johnson remarked, "We still feel very strongly that the initial team meeting needs to be face to face." She's right. This team was smart enough to recognize that teams that travel build InTouch best. The way they created their War eRoom enhanced relationships and collaboration to a new level.

The way the people at Chute Gerdeman introduced and used their 24/7 eCollaboration technology with clients and with each other puts them not only at the cutting edge, but also in the winner's circle with their clients. Their result is no accident; it was part of their plan to improve InTouch, from afar.

Create an eCommunication Plan with Individuals

Creating InTouch from afar is critical for your own personal success. Every leader, team, or individual has a small, but specific, list of individuals with whom we want to create and grow InTouch, from afar.

One individual might be a distant boss. According to the Meetings in America III study by WorldCom, one out of three either manage people who are somewhere else, or are managed by someone who is somewhere else. Few will dispute the importance of building trust with one's superior, communicating frequently, and keeping her in the loop.

> *Every leader, team, or individual has a small, but specific list, of individuals with whom we want to create and grow InTouch, from afar.*

Another individual might be a distant peer. Ninety-seven percent of us must collaborate with others to do our work. Today, people are commonly placed in high dependency relationships, yet rarely see each other. We need to create InTouch from afar so that we can work well together and be responsive to each other.

A third example is a distant customer, partner, or key person high in the organization. We need to create InTouch so that the relationship flourishes, without travel.

InTouch with these key individuals is too important to be left to a random thought. To build InTouch effectively, Bionic eTeams create a plan with one purpose: build the relationship. The plan will be unique to the relationship, the technology, and the nature of the collaboration.

Anthony Robbins, President of SGI Federal, is a Bionic eLeader. His organization spans locations from Washington, D.C., to Silicon Valley, California. His team has only a few days of face time a year. Despite distance, he has inspired his virtual organization to record-breaking success, because he personalizes a plan to be InTouch when people are virtual.

> "Without a plan, leaders get interrupted by the urgency of the moment, it takes away from my ability to lead my team."

Robbins doesn't just have phone conversations; he creates connections. He doesn't just find out what other people's interests are; he finds a way to connect himself into that person's world. He doesn't just respond to questions in town hall meetings; he connects himself to that person or some news that happened in that local environment. He is constantly casting out links to create an intricate Web of connections that are designed to enhance the quality of InTouch.

When a team spends most of its time apart, it easily can get out of touch. Leaders become very reactive in their communication, communicating only when there is a crisis. As a Bionic eLeader, Robbins knows that communication is too important to leave to chance. So he has a communication plan to create InTouch with each of the key people he relies on most.

Robbins said, "Without a plan, leaders get sidetracked. If I don't have a plan, and I allow myself to get interrupted by the urgency of the moment, it takes away from my ability to lead my team."

Robbins' communication plan has four parts:

1. *Frequency.* How frequently does this person need communication from me?
2. *Duration.* How long do we need to communicate?
3. *Content.* What will we talk about?
4. *Media.* What media does this person prefer?

Now, if you are already mentally drawing out your form to distribute by e-mail to the people you depend on most, hold on! You'll get a very different result than this model Bionic eLeader. Robbins is absolutely committed to building strong interpersonal relationships with each and every one of the people on his team. When some work down the hall and others work thousands of miles away, no general plan or Q&A sheet will do.

> *"Otherwise, a leader risks creating an artificial relationship that just won't stand up when tough times happen."*

Each of his direct reports has a different personality, a different style, and a different communication preference. So, Robbins crafts a *customized* plan for each person on his direct team. Robbins said, "Communication needs are different for each of my direct reports, and that is important. Some who are right down the hall may need less frequency than those who are distant. When it comes to communication, I want to keep my direct reports inside their comfort zone. I want each to be comfortable being led."

If it sounds like creating all of those individual communication plans is time consuming, it is. Robbins says that it takes about 90 days to figure out clearly what plan he needs to institute to lead and manage a new team member. But it is worth the time, and the payoffs are significant.

Robbins continues, "If you get to know the people, you'll get to understand what drives them, what motivates them, and how to communicate with them. You'll know how they want to lead and how they want to be led." That's when he completes his customized plan. "Otherwise, a leader risks creating an artificial relationship that just won't stand up when tough times happen."

Robbins sent some messages to his leadership team in the same media, but the most important ones—the ones that were critical to his relationship with each person—were personalized.

Create an eCommunication Plan for the Team

Members of a Bionic eTeam expect to be first on the list of any communication that applies to the whole team. This communication includes changes, such as changes in personnel, in the organization, in the team's work, in deadlines, in milestones, in supplier status, in production status—this list could go on for a long time. Other team communication includes announcements, action item progress, adjustments in the project plan, real-time production output, and more.

> Every team has core information that everyone on the team needs to know.

Every team has core information that everyone on the team needs to know. If everyone on the team receives the information in the same way and at the same time, InTouch builds. The greatest pitfall about all-team communication, however, is when some find out before others, which breaks InTouch.

To build InTouch, Bionic eTeams have a plan for communication that makes sure everyone is first on the list. Take Rory, a manufacturing manager for a major computer company. Manufacturing for their product occurred in Colorado, Mexico City, and Singapore.

The company was going through several reorganizations—all impacting manufacturing in all three locations. To preserve InTouch, the executive management of the company created and stuck to a specific communication plan. Any major announcement that directly impacted manufacturing was made to all sites, timed to occur at precisely 4 PM Colorado time, Monday through Thursday. That time translates to 5 PM in Mexico City and 7 AM the next day in Singapore. The result is that everyone on the team received those critical announcements during their normal workday.

> To build InTouch, Bionic eTeams have a plan for communication that makes sure everyone is first on the list.

The eTeam communication plan needs to fit the team, but always be designed to create InTouch. Some teams create a matrix that specifically identifies who gets what communication, via which media, using which distribution list. Others specify what words to use in subject lines, so people can archive and organize the e-mail better. Still others specify how to handle urgent communication and escalations.

To evolve to Bionic eTeamwork, however, the eCommunication plan will include ways to create InTouch through collaborative technology, such as Web conference technology and eTeamroom technology, which you will read more about later in this book. Importantly, these tools do not create teamwork. How your team uses them does. The eCommunication plan puts organization around how to use tools to improve InTouch.

> Tools do not create teamwork. How your team uses them does.

Have a Plan to Keep Your Extended eTeam InTouch

Every eTeam has a broad array of people that it counts on for success, which can include:

* The entire company

- A whole business unit
- An extended team, one or more steps out from the core team
- The team sponsors that work half a world away
- The associates from the eTeam's partnerships and alliances
- And more . . . .

Bionic eTeams know that keeping these critical eTeam members informed is not enough. Instead, they need to have a plan to enhance InTouch with people on the extended team.

The eCommunication plan for the eOrganization should follow a similar format to the one you create for your Bionic eTeam.

Create a Precise Detailed Plan for International eTeams

Teams that span one culture are constantly challenged to keep trust high. Teams that span the world are in a league of their own. Multiculture teams need a precise plan to ensure that relationships build across cultures.

If the slippery slope for one-culture teams is 30 degrees, the slope for multiculture teams is 80 degrees (nearly straight down). In multiculture teams, when trust is broken, the results are far more devastating than on single-culture teams.

The best defense is a strong offense—to set up a clear foundation so trust can flourish, not be eroded, when communicating virtually.

> *Bionic eTeams have a plan to enhance InTouch with people on the extended team.*

Building on the foundation that you learned in the last chapter, the HP LaserJet-Canon Team achieved exceptional levels of trust—by design. General Manager Neil Martini says, "We have a highly structured process that defines when to meet, what to talk about in meetings, how to escalate an issue, and other key issues. This process is well thought-out and has stood the test of time. *Nothing is left to chance.*"

Communication across dramatically different cultures is too fragile and critical to be done only when people think about it or when one has time. Bionic eLeaders always have a well thought-out plan, and they stay close to their plan to build trust across cultures.

> *The best defense is a strong offense— to set up a clear foundation so trust can flourish, not be eroded, when communicating virtually.*

In the earlier years of the HP/Canon alliance, video teleconferencing was not available. Now they have it and use it regularly. Their video teleconference rooms have separate screens to project the people, the graphics, and the documentation of the decision process. This team created and used a decision process that both their Japanese and U.S. members are comfortable with. In the Japanese culture, people tend not to be very direct, especially if they do not agree. If people from the U.S. culture seemed confrontational, the Japanese members would shy away. So they jointly created a way to address the issues. Most important, they developed a clear way to know when there was closure on an issue.

Trust, when virtual, was critical to the success of the HP LaserJet-Canon Team. The time and energy invested in laying the foundation for building In-

> *Nothing is left to chance.*

Touch were resources well spent. The HP LaserJet-Canon team was successful because they attended to the virtual communication that transformed them into a very successful, cohesive partnership.

Their focus on building trusting relationships was a top priority, not something people did when they had time. Their partnership transcended corporate boundaries and immense cultural differences because of their priority on getting InTouch. They did. And the rest is history.

A Few Final Words . . .

Can an eTeam or individuals that collaborate from afar create InTouch without travel?

- Yes, if the team members already have positive relationships, perhaps from previous work.

- Yes, if the team is working on a short-term assignment that produces a tangible value, but is not the only factor that one's career depends on.

- Yes, if the team or individuals have effective best practices on new technologies (like internet conference technology) and know how to create a high-trust eMeeting environment.

- Yes, with new best practices and new technologies, if the eTeam members' intent and actions are consistently trusting.

- Yes, if both have the intent and effort to connect. Creating solid levels of InTouch may take a little longer, but it can work.

InTouch tends to happen significantly faster when an onsite visit happens first, but travel is not always critical. New methods and new technology (like Web conferencing and electronic teamrooms) dramatically improve the quality of relationship-creating communication that people can share while apart.

B I O N I C

eTeamwork Checklist

Build InTouch, Virtually

This chapter began with the quote, *"I like the freedom of being remote. But I can't stand being ignored."*

Relationships when people are not in one place are too important to be left to chance. So Bionic eLeaders make sure the eTeam has a clear plan to ensure that trust is built, not eroded, when people communicate virtually.

Bionic eTeams build InTouch to significantly higher levels through the use of collaborative technology. It is critical that teams establish, and then embrace, a plan to use Web conference technology and electronic teamroom technology, at minimum, to speed collaboration, interaction, and trust.

Focus your Bionic eTeamwork communication plan on ways people will create InTouch when apart. Use technology to improve collaboration and communication while reducing travel. Build InTouch at several levels:

❏ With individuals, from afar

❏ With the virtual team, from afar

❏ With your boss or team leader, from afar

❏ With your international team, from afar, paying close attention to identifying ways to bridge the distance between cultures and languages

❏ In eTeams that can't travel

❏ Among individuals who must collaborate, from afar

THINGS YOU CAN DO TODAY TO
Build InTouch, Virtually

eLeaders	eTeams	Individuals
Create a plan for how you build trust in yourself from afar, which includes: • How quickly you respond to eCommunication. • How accessible you make yourself to all eTeam members at all locations. • How you build connections from afar. • How you demonstrate integrity from afar. • How you use eMeetings to build and reinforce team spirit.	Create a plan to increase sense of team from afar, which includes: • Best practices to enhance sense of team in eMeetings. • Best practices for managing eTeam responsiveness among members. • Best practices to handle and resolve problems. • Best practices for managing key eTeam communication. • Best practices and norms for increasing human bonds from afar.	Even though you may not use "teammate" to refer to the people with whom you communicate regularly from afar, make them feel like a teammate. Create a plan to build that warmth, which includes: • Response expectations others can count on from you. • Ways you communicate virtually that build warmth and interaction. • Overt ways to build bonds with you from afar.

The Heart of Bionic eTeamwork

Human Moments of Truth, Not Vision

> All men need something greater than themselves to look up to and worship. They must be able to touch the divine here on earth.
>
> **Sir Francis Walsingham**
> The Movie: *Elizabeth*

"D id any of you get a message from the President on your voice mail this morning?" said Sandra, as she entered a room where 15 of her peers had gathered for a weekly meeting. All were project managers working for a major telecommunications company in the middle of great change. All were very dedicated people who had devoted tremendous effort and time to make their projects successful. All were under continual stress to fight for the money, executive support, and political support to make their projects successful.

Yes, everyone had received the same voice message in their voice mailboxes. None had received a message from the President before, so initially the surprise of getting a message from such a high-level person generated a lot of talk.

The President's message informed everyone in the company about the company's new direction. He defined the new vision: "By the year 2000, to be the finest company in the world connecting people with their world." Can you guess the reaction of other project managers? Do you think this phrase suddenly vaulted them into extraordinary performance? Do you think it provided them that human piece that was lacking in their organization?

Instantly, cynicism set in. One said, "I wonder how much money the executive team spent on some consultants at some lavish resort to come up with those words?" In a cutting tone, followed by an audible tisk, another said, "The finest company? Right!" Still another said, "Connecting people with their world? What does that mean I am supposed to do?" Their company had a history of being very technology focused, not human focused. These words were like throwing salt on a very deep wound.

> For Bionic eTeams, success begins by creating a close, highly relevant sense of human community.

Visions are important for business success, as are strategy, mission, goals, and value statements. As you can see from the project manager's meeting, though, the lofty words, although written like a poet, failed to inspire. The disconnect between the feeling the executives tried to create versus what they actually created could fill the Grand Canyon. Lofty words shared from a distance often don't translate well. They're too "remote."

For Bionic eTeams, success begins by creating a close, highly relevant sense of *human* community that people find through winning business and making customers happy. With today's geographically split teams, no manager can wander around enough to create this community. No vision, mission, or objectives statement can inspire this community, either. All these traditional management tools are important. By themselves, however, they fail to drive inspired performance in eTeam members, especially those that work in isolation from the eLeader and other eTeam members.

The way most visions, missions, goals, and charters are written and shared are too removed from the heart and soul of why people work. They're also too removed from what people look for as a result of their work, on a deep human level. It doesn't matter if your team produces a product, delivers a service, or performs any other kind of business function.

If you want inspired performance, people need to be InTouch with the humanity of serving customers and making customers happy. People need to be InTouch with the excitement of winning business together without working together in one place. More specifically, eTeams need to focus on the *key behaviors* that are most critical in creating success globally as members of an energized, focused eTeam.

In a team or organization, everyone either serves a customer directly or serves a customer indirectly. If they don't, that person either isn't connected or isn't necessary. Bionic eLeaders adroitly make sure people's daily focus and daily work *is* totally connected to the magic of serving customers.

Moments of Truth

So, what piece is missing from the traditional management tool kit that connects an eTeam on a human level? It's focusing on the Moments of Truth—an amazingly simple, yet powerful concept that Jan Carlzon used to focus and transform his dispersed organization, with amazing results. His was a service team, but this same concept works for all teams. Moments of Truth focus on specific behaviors that—at critical moments in time—create eTeam success. Let's learn about how Carlzon used this concept to transform his organization, then expand on it with other teams.

When Jan Carlzon became CEO of SAS airlines years ago, he had vision to make SAS "the best airline for the frequent business traveler." There must have been more than a few snickers initially at Carlzon's pie in the sky vision. When he took over, the company was $20 million in the red and stuck in a limited, competitive marketplace.

Twelve months later, Carlzon had transformed the company's loss into a $54 million gain—a positive change of $74 million! His company spanned locations all over Europe and the world.

Carlzon was successful because he put heart and soul back in the company, not just through vision, but through Moments of Truth. The vision had a lofty sound, to be "the best . . . ," but that statement was far too vague to transform the company. People couldn't wrap their arms around it. Vision statements are important. Even in a high-trust corporate culture, however, visions often aren't tangible enough to motivate and rapidly change behavior of every employee in a geographically dispersed organization.

> *Moments of Truth are designed to focus people on what to do that will lead the eTeam to the highest level of success.*

Moments of Truth, on the other hand, focus on specific and tangible behaviors. Behaviors win customers, and behaviors turn customers away. Behaviors create success, and behaviors create failure. Moments of Truth act as a constant, effective guide that can be used as a self-feedback tool. They are designed to focus people on what to do that will lead the eTeam to the highest level of success. Moments of Truth make building success very personal and doable.

Think about the last time you traveled on an airplane as a customer. Hopefully, you have experienced positive Moments of Truth that made you feel valued as an airline passenger. Maybe it was the moment the reservationist went the extra mile to get you on a critical flight. It could have been the moment the gate agent gave you a free upgrade because it was your birthday. Or perhaps it was a flight attendant that happily gave you an aspirin from her purse, because there were none in the cabin. Positive Moments of Truth like these warm the experience of travel and make you want to choose that airline again.

In contrast, maybe your Moments of Truth made you never want to travel with that airline again. Maybe it was the moment your checked luggage finally made it to baggage claim, one hour after arrival, smashed to smithereens. Maybe it was the way the flight attendants engaged in loud, almost party-talk conversation, while ignoring you and other passengers in the cabin. Or maybe it was the moment you plugged into the airplane's sound system, only to find that your seat's connection to it was not working, nor was the reading light. Moments of Truth like these make travel as cold as the metal on the outside of the airplane at 38,000 feet!

Moments of Truth acted like a magnifying glass, helping Carlzon focus everyone in the organization on what each had to *do* to build a dramatic level of success at SAS. If vision and mission and goals are the *what's,* Moments of Truth are the *how's.* Carlzon's Moments of Truth focused his people on the human experience of being a customer of SAS. Moments of Truth happened every time an SAS employee interfaced directly or indirectly with an SAS customer.

In fact, Carlzon said that 50,000 Moments of Truth happened every day at SAS. Carlzon used Moments of Truth to change random acts of excellence into consistent, consciously created acts of excellence by everyone in the company. They guide people not to do work mindlessly, but rather to reflect on what each is doing at the Moment of Truth, when behaviors have the greatest impact on success.

> *Moments of Truth guide people not to do work mindlessly, but rather to reflect on what each is doing when behaviors have the greatest impact on success.*

It doesn't matter if the Moment of Truth happens directly or indirectly from one human being to another. Moments of Truth have an impact. As an airline customer, if you have a choice, which Moments of Truth will you gravitate toward? Of course, the positive ones! The winning approach was to make flying SAS not just an airline, but rather a human experience that surpassed all others, filled with positive Moments of Truth that made business customers feel special. Carlzon launched a campaign titled "People Pleasing Planes." The backbone to that campaign was Moments of Truth—the specific behaviors that SAS people had to consistently *do* to create People Pleasing Planes.

As you read earlier, SAS's financial turnaround in that year was impressive. Moments of Truth quickly transformed Carlzon's company from being a technology (a plane that flew people from one location to another) to a human experience that directly made the company successful.

Many would be happy enough to produce the financial turnaround, but Carlzon got another gigantic bonus. As the people in SAS focused on the Moments of Truth, morale skyrocketed. People want to do good work. Getting InTouch with customers is inspiring. Moments of Truth guided people to do great work and feel better about it. It was a brilliant way to help everyone in SAS focus constantly on the human side of airline travel. In a globally dispersed setting, no manager can physically wander around enough to create this kind of focus. Moments of Truth fill the void when the manager cannot be there.

> *In a globally dispersed setting, no manager can physically wander around enough to create this kind of focus.*

Moments of Truth are the heart of Bionic eTeamwork. They gave SAS airlines a heart by getting everyone InTouch with the human side of providing air transportation. They gave the employees a heart by focusing on behaviors around customers. They gave the company a healthy heart by providing a structure to keep morale high. The result was that customers could rely on a unified, customer-focused Scandinavian Airlines "face" or presence, no matter where in the world customers interacted with SAS. Moments of Truth filled the feedback vacuum that exists when team members work in a different location than the leader or each other.

Moments of Truth for Manufacturing Teams

Moments of Truth aren't just effective for service teams. They are equally as effective for product teams, manufacturing teams, project teams, technical teams, and other teams that are typically considered "nonservice." Every team has Moments of Truth that will make it successful. Bionic eLeaders use Moments of Truth to align people on the behaviors and attitudes that are critical for success.

Take one organization that manufactured custom blood tubing sets for open heart surgery. At the beginning of this story, their product carried a premium price tag, but was delivered with poor quality and poor service. High in the organization, conversations were in process to shut this group down. The company had a common salesforce that sold 14 other products in the brand. This product, however, was so bad that sales trainers told new salespeople, "Don't sell the blood tubing sets. Our other company products are great, but the blood tubing set products will get you into trouble with customers." How would you like to find out about that statement a week or so into your new job as leader of the Blood Tubing Set eTeam?

By the end of this story, the blood tubing set team had the fastest growing product in the company. Its percent of profitability and its net profit to the bottom line doubled. The operation was expanded, including a successful manufacturing operation in Europe. This eTeam became the model for other parts of the company.

How did this eLeader transform the group so powerfully— and *fast?* He used Moments of Truth to focus people on what they had to do to be successful.

Manufacturing traditionally operates as its own entity, separate and removed from everyone else, including customers. This manufacturing operation was no exception. Its singular focus was internally driven: cut costs and meet schedules. With an ever growing list of new competitors springing up around the world, their internal focus was killing them in the marketplace.

One of the key complaints was that this organization was unresponsive to customers. For example, it could take six months to one year for a customer to see even the most minor change reflected in their customized blood tubing set. The company was so focused on their internally driven manufacturing procedures and practices, that customers were regularly told, "No, we can't do that." When people from this organization hung up the phone, the transaction was out of their mind."

Jim Kutsko, the manufacturing manager, launched a campaign to focus his organization on a new Moment of Truth: *Give customers what they want.* He said, "If we focus on giving the customers what they want, the question can no longer be, 'Can we do it?' Instead the question must become 'How we can do it?'" The Moment of Truth helped Kutsko focus the whole operation on the customer versus making the internal team comfortable.

> *"If we focus on giving the customers what they want, the question can no longer be, 'Can we do it?' Instead the question must become 'How we can do it?'"*

Kutsko spent most of his day focusing people on the new Moment of Truth. He conducted many meetings about it, many discussions in the hall, and many reminders that were placed visibly for all people in all locations to see. He brought customers to the facility or linked them in by phone, so that everyone heard the words directly from the customer's mouth.

Kutsko said, "The focus on giving customers what they wanted was terrific. It focused everyone on the customer. It helped people understand what customers wanted. Customers wanted quality products, customized to their needs. They wanted our products competitively priced. And they wanted our products when they needed them, on the customer's timeline. This was just about the opposite of the way it had been done."

The new focus paid off in a constant stream of ways. As part of the customer agreement, each hospital held a three-month inventory, and so did Kutsko's group. He said, "If the customer complained, we would check our inventory to see if other packs we were storing for them had the same problem. Even if they had a minor complaint, we sent out replacement inventory immediately, and asked them to return their stock to us."

Kutsko's team did this even if the customer said that the problem "was no big deal." Now, instead of resolving the problem over six months, any problem the customer stated was gone in two weeks. The team reworked the returned inventory. To accounting, this process didn't make sense. But the results of this team show that it obviously did.

Focusing on the Moment of Truth guided everyone to examine how he "gave customers what they wanted." With Moment of Truth's strong focus, the stories came streaming in. The one Kutsko is happiest to tell is when one of the salespersons called on the famous heart surgeon, Dr. Michael DeBakey. When a hospital placed an order for a sample custom tubing set for open heart surgery, the process normally had taken one week. Kutsko said, "We knew we had arrived when we delivered a sample pack to DeBakey in only one day."

For over two years, Kutsko's group had tried to do business with Dr. DeBakey. Because their manufacturing organization gave DeBakey what he wanted, the team got the order. In the process, they created a happy and loyal new customer. Moments of Truth have a clear message: Pay attention to me! Focus on me! I will help you be successful. Moments of Truth are powerful tools to keep people focused all the time, anywhere.

> *Well integrated Moments of Truth become deeply imbedded in the corporate culture.*

Moments of Truth work. Sometimes Moments of Truth span product and service, such as Tandem's *Nonstop* (computers and service to keep the computers running without stopping), or Ford's *Quality Is Job 1* (all levels of Ford Motor Company). Well integrated Moments of Truth become deeply imbedded in the corporate culture, like FedEx's *Absolutely Positively Overnight,* and Lexus' *Relentless Pursuit of Perfection.* Moments of Truth don't sit in filing drawers. Nor are they empty slogans. Instead, Moments of Truth are a way of working, getting things done, and winning business. They are a powerful foundation for a culture of excellence to create success unconstrained by location.

Leadership from Afar: Why Moments of Truth Work

Teams that work virtually don't have the same focusing mechanisms that colocated teams do. Almost every traditional leadership technique managers have learned is designed for people that work right outside the door, not halfway around the world. Manage by Wandering Around. (It used to take seconds; now it takes hours just to get there.) Catch people doing things right, in the moment. (We used to see it; from afar, we don't.) Give immediate feedback. (We used to know right away; now we find out days later.) Keep people motivated. (We used to see what they needed and when they needed it; now it seems like a guessing game.)

People who work across distance exist in a feedback vacuum. As one team member said, "I work in a location with about 100 other people who are employed by my company. My desk is smack dab in the middle. I may as well have a desk in the middle of the desert. I'm the only one at my location that is part of this team. The team leader and everyone else are hundreds and thousands of miles away from me and from each other. I come here to this site to work every day. Eight hours or so later, I leave. No one at my location really knows or cares about what I'm doing, how hard I work, or what I have achieved. The sad part is, the leader and the team don't know these things either." The problem is more than a failure in leadership. It is a failure to focus on the Moment of Truth.

A person in this same environment, InTouch with the Moment of Truth, will have a very different experience.

Despite the isolation, the need for a focusing mechanism is strong, if not stronger, when the team is virtual. In that person's local environment are thousands of distractions, baggage that holds them back or keeps them in "the wrong place" for success. Unfortunately, the feedback mechanisms that could change behavior are almost nonexistent.

The good news is that Moments of Truth almost magically fill that void. And here's why. Integrated properly, the concept provides a steady stream of powerful, immediate feedback, which dramatically surpasses generalities like "being the best . . ." or "increase revenues by. . . ." It provides a constant flow of tangible, specific feedback that is powerful at a visual level, a feeling level, and a hearing level. With Mo-

> With Moments of Truth, powerful feedback occurs every time a person interacts with a customer or impacts a customer.

ments of Truth, feedback is constant. Feedback is specific. Feedback is accurate. The bonus is that powerful feedback occurs every time a person interacts with a customer or impacts a customer.

Let's look at the SAS example. Their Moments of Truth focused on behaviors that created People Pleasing Planes. First, Carlzon helped people to understand what People Pleasing Planes looked like, and why that image was critical for success. Then, he wanted people throughout all sites and all functions of the airline to take a closer look at what they were doing to create People Pleasing Planes.

If 55 percent of our ability to understand and to create rapport comes from visual cues, look at the impact of Moments of Truth. Employees had interactions with customers all day long. Moments of Truth acted like a magnifying glass on employee behaviors. They sharpened every employee's focus on what customers were looking for when flying SAS. They forced employees to take a closer look at their own behavior with customers. They enabled employees to see and to judge their own behavior, then make visible corrections in the moment. Eventually, they enabled SAS to deliver a distinctly consistent level of quality service that people would see when flying their airline.

Second, 25 percent of our ability to understand comes from feeling cues. Moments of Truth were tangible. Customers felt them. SAS employees felt them. They increased the sense of unity and pride in the uniqueness of the service SAS people were delivering. Feedback was now specific, concrete, immediate—constant, across all employees and locations.

People became more sensitive to the feeling they were creating in their interaction with customers. When they saw their behavior create smiles instead of angry words, not only did the customer feel better, but the SAS employee felt better, too. In the absence of specific and concrete feedback from a leader or team member, Moments of Truth enabled each SAS employee to give herself effective and immediate feedback, based on real criteria that were critical for success.

Third, 20 percent of our ability to understand comes from audio cues. Moments of Truth generate a multitude of conversations between distant managers and distant team members. People defined them, analyzed them, and celebrated them. Moments of Truth became the number one topic of conversation within SAS. But the most important conversation is the one that occurs in the Moment of Truth itself. Moments of Truth give people immediate feedback on those conversations. Human nature encourages people to be in harmony with the world around them, so Moments of Truth generate those internal conversations that matter.

Moments of Truth are not a panacea. They're not a one-shot deal where an eLeader says a few words, and then the words are never talked about again. Neither is the program a catchy phrase or theme that is created on the fly or printed on some banner near the exit door. Quite the contrary. *Moments of Truth become the central conversation around which eTeam collaboration is linked.* It's a conversation that Bionic eLeaders keep in front of people, ongoing.

The bottom line in Moments of Truth is that the program is designed to help employees do the right work, and feel great about it. The more specific and concrete Bionic eLeaders are in articulating (or helping the eTeam articulate) *how* to create success, the happier our people will be. Moments of Truth give us a specific language of words and behaviors that binds us as a human community through our global work. They give us a common understanding of what is important to please customers around the world. Unlike vision statements that often get forgotten, Moments of Truth are real and relevant. People review them at the beginning of the day, when interacting with customers during the day, and again at the end of day.

Finally, when Moments of Truth are articulated, they become the center of how we build a sense of team, how we focus leader coaching, how we decide what we need to learn, how we prioritize what processes need to change, and how we stay focused on the right things every day.

Even without technology, Moments of Truth are designed to provide clear, specific, and immediate feedback on virtually everything an employee does throughout the day. Rather than waiting three weeks for the next time the eLeader visits your site, you get feedback immediately. Moments of Truth enable people to give themselves a constant stream of accurate, timely self-feedback. It fills a huge feedback gap. Moments of Truth are there when the leader is not.

> *Rather than waiting three weeks for the next time the eLeader visits your site, you get feedback immediately.*

Driving Moments of Truth with 24/7 Technology

Many eTeams, however, are looking for an even higher level of driving Moments of Truth with technology. How do eLeaders accelerate Moments of Truth across larger organizations? Is it possible to ramp up the focus on Moments of Truth so that you have hundreds or thousands or tens of thousands delivering consistent Moments of Truth to your customers?

The answer is yes.

Howard Sorgen is Chief Technology Officer of Merrill Lynch's U.S. International and Private Banking Groups. With all the wisdom that comes with knowing the power of technology, yet understanding the human needs of groups, he has created truly Bionic eTeamwork at Merrill Lynch. He has also created a new standard for financial services and speed. Sorgen led a major initiative, centered around Moments of Truth, which integrates technology with human behavior to serve customers at dramatically higher levels.

Most financial services companies call their frontline people brokers, financial advisors, broker agents, financial consultants, and similar professional names. Merrill Lynch, however, saw their success differently. In their quest to be the premier global financial services firm, they took a distinctly human approach—they talked with their customers and their consultants.

Based on that information, they created their Moment of Truth: Trusted Global Advisor. Whether the customers are small businesses, big businesses, or independent investors, Merrill Lynch wanted them to view its employees not just as global advisors; rather, as *trusted* global advisors. Trust is clearly at the forefront.

In the many focus groups that followed within Merrill Lynch, Trusted Global Advisor (TGA) created a lot of excitement. When the initiative started, Sorgen said, the consultants were told, "Assume that technology can do everything. What would you want to do to serve your clients better?" Notice that the focus is not on technology as the solution. At this point, the focus is clearly on the Moment of Truth: Trusted Global Advisor.

> *The technology team did not develop the technology in a vacuum and roll it out in a grand program one year later.*

As he and his team traveled around the country, Sorgen emphasized to the consultants, "This is your system. It's not something that's being done by technologists and management. This is your system, and we want it to be whatever will help you serve our client base." This was a wise approach. One key reason technology fails is because the people who will use it are excluded from the development process. Sorgen's group built the technology based on the business requirements voiced by the financial consultants then delivered it according to the latter's priorities.

Importantly, the technology team did not develop the technology in a vacuum and roll it out in a grand program one year later. Quite the contrary. Instead, their process was iterative every step of the way. As each new part was designed, Sorgen's group took it back to test teams for feedback, asking, "Is this what you want? Is this the way you want to see it?"

Then, based on that feedback, Sorgen's team would modify or rebuild it as needed. This process continued on an ongoing basis until they knew they had sufficient feedback to know that they were doing it right. Once the technology was right, Sorgen provided training so people used 100 percent of its power, not just the usual 10 percent that most of us know about the technologies we use daily.

When the first rollout was completed in June of 1997, the Trusted Global Advisor workstation didn't just sit unused on people's desktops. People used it, eagerly and willingly, and with great speed. Sorgen said he was amazed by how quickly people in the organization figured out they could collaborate better with clients. "We believe that in order to help our clients make money, we have been on a mission to combine the investment savvy of the consultant with technology—and that creates a Bionic eTeam. From our perspective, that has been our goal. When we put that technology out, employees realized how quickly they could do more than they could themselves."

Currently, 14,500 financial consultants are using this system. They're serving 5.5 million individual investors, helping them achieve wealth so they can fulfill their hopes and dreams. Merrill Lynch measures productivity gains by the way financial consultants manage their time and their clients' time. Trusted Global Advisors have measured 30 to 40 percent productivity gains, not just for their consultants, but also for their busy clientele.

Armed with the power of technology, Merrill Lynch's Trusted Global Advisors are better able to accelerate trust with customers. With a brilliant rollout, they can serve their clients with all their Bionic parts. In the morning, they are briefed via Web conference by key fund analysts in New York. They hear "right from the horse's mouth" exactly what's hot and what's not.

Later that day, when consultants talk to clients, they can say, "This morning our top analyst on this fund said . . . ." Consultants can quickly and easily send articles by e-mail to clients that are targeted to building trust. The TGA system creates truly trusted global advisors, powerfully charged to serve clients. Bionic, they're infinitely more empowered to create and grow trust with large numbers of clients, and give every one the attention and customization each wants.

BIONIC
eTeamwork Checklist

How to Create Moments of Truth

This chapter began with a quote from one of my favorite movies, *Elizabeth. "All men need something greater than themselves to look up to and worship. They must be able to touch the divine here on earth."*

eTeams exist in a feedback vacuum. The leader is somewhere else. eTeam members are somewhere else. It is a tough place to stay focused and feel positive.

Human nature drives us to seek connections and to seek meaning in what we do. Although we may not be able to touch the divine, we do need to touch something greater than ourselves. Our hearts are happy when we become part of something that makes the world a little brighter, a little happier, a little better. *Every time we touch a Moment of Truth, we touch a happier, brighter place.*

Bionic eLeaders and eTeams use Moments of Truth to get InTouch with the human side of their work, and then keep it alive. A Moment of Truth isn't some far off vision or long-term goal. Instead, it is clear, specific, and tangible, filling the feedback vacuum that drains eTeams of their spirit.

Getting InTouch with human Moments of Truth that build real eTeam success, virtually, is fun and fulfilling. Isolate the five key behaviors that enable the highest level of success in your eTeam. Crisp the words down into five short statements. Then be creative in keeping their direction alive in the following five ways:

- ☐ Team members receive continuous self-feedback, in the absence of the team leader.

- ☐ Leaders coach and mentor from afar.

- ☐ Sense of team across distance improves.

- ☐ Key learning is identified from afar.

- ☐ Changes occur in processes, technology, or the organization itself.

THINGS YOU CAN DO TODAY TO
Create Moments of Truth

eLeaders	eTeams	Individuals
Help your eTeam tap into its human side by leading the creation of Moments of Truth to drive success worldwide.	Work with the eLeader to create Moments of Truth to drive eTeam success worldwide.	If you are a person who works alone, set your own personal Moments of Truth.

eLeaders

Help your eTeam tap into its human side by leading the creation of Moments of Truth to drive success worldwide.

- List no more than five specific behaviors (usually with customers) that deliver the highest return in creating team results.
- Then create a communication plan to leverage those words worldwide to drive excitement, momentum, and team spirit when people are not in one place.
- Use Moments of Truth in eMeetings, etc., in ways that celebrate and build eTeam success.

eTeams

Work with the eLeader to create Moments of Truth to drive eTeam success worldwide.

- Once they are created, post the Moments of Truth in an eSpace that you see every day.
- Review the Moments of Truth throughout the day to keep yourself focused on behaviors that make a difference.
- Share your successes with your eTeam leader.
- Share your methods with your eTeammates.

Individuals

If you are a person who works alone, set your own personal Moments of Truth.

- Reflect on the five key behaviors that you do every day that yield the highest results.
- Post them by your computer, and review them every day.
- Use them to stay focused on doing the right things that produce the highest results.
- At the end of the day, post at least one positive thought about the result the Moment of Truth generated that day.

C H A P T E R

eMotion

Building Sense of Team, from Afar

> *Leaders can't create connectedness. Rather, believe
> that it is already there. Then look for ways to facilitate
> that connectedness.*
>
> **George Davis**
> Davis and Deane

I n only three short years, a high-tech service company
based in California grew from 3 people to over 800. Employees were dispersed throughout North America, South
America, and Europe. About half of the people worked in formal office buildings at headquarters. The rest worked from
cars, hotels, home offices, and other virtual locations around
the world.

The company couldn't have done a better job of having the
right niche in the right marketplace. The corporate atmosphere
was fast, aggressive, and filled with pressure. The company
paid high salaries and offered exciting technical challenges
that attracted highly motivated people. People willingly worked
60-hour weeks because there weren't enough people to fill all
of the job vacancies. Within the next six months, the company's employee roster looked like it would double again in
size—that is, if it could find enough qualified people to fill all
the vacancies.

To manage the rapid growth, the executive staff decided that they needed to communicate more with the people in the organization. An employee survey showed that people in all of the worldwide locations felt out of touch. A paper newsletter that came out once every three months was far too slow. By the time the words were printed on paper, everything had changed. Some news was relayed by e-mail, but only the managers received it. Some managers relayed the information in their eTeam conference calls, but others didn't. The result was an eRumor mill that was running rampant with distorted information.

> *Nearly two-thirds of the employees dialed in by phone. Thirty minutes later, over half had dropped off.*

With all the publicity about town hall meetings in the news, the executives chose to hold an all hands meeting via a conference call. The purpose of the one-hour eMeeting was to help the organization get connected. To do that, each of the five executives gave a ten-minute status report. Status is the right word, as the reports recited dry, forgetable numbers and information at a monotonously slow pace. The eMeeting was a business meeting, designed to share information, nothing more. With fact after fact, projection after projection, the presentations droned on. The final ten minutes of the call were left for questions and answers from the field.

The first all hands conference attracted a lot of attention. Nearly two-thirds of the employees dialed in by phone. Thirty minutes later, over half had dropped off. At the end of the call, only two people asked questions in the Q&A session. The next month, fewer than 10 percent of the people dialed in. At the end, when the moderator asked if there were any questions, the only sound the executives and call participants heard was complete and total silence from the field. This group of executives had no idea why their all hands meeting hadn't worked.

The eMeeting had failed because it lacked eMotion from afar.

eMotion: Inspiring the Troops from Afar

Anyone who has ever been on a traditional high-performance team knows that the experience is a very emotional event. People discover each other's humanity, which makes them bond with one another on many different levels. Within the team, people feel the excitement of challenge, the warmth of working together, the joy of creating an excellent result, the fun of the creativity, and the list goes on. It's a place filled with immense complexity, tough work, endless change, long hours, high frustration, tight deadlines, and impossible requirements. If the joy is in the journey, so are laughter, anxiety, tears, and pain. There is no way in the world that the experience will be devoid of emotion as people pull together to the finish line.

> Anyone who has ever been on a traditional high-performance team knows that the experience is a very emotional event.

When the high performance team finally finishes its work—the product is launched, the project is complete, the key milestone is met—a celebration is in order. Everyone on the team wants to be together to toast their great work, celebrate their new relationships, and to cheer their success. They want to rehash the journey, their personal growth, and the emotional journey of making it to the end successfully. They pat each other on the back for stepping forward and helping each other with the right ideas at just the right time. For most teams, this isn't the first time they've had these conversations. Every time they met during work and outside of work, these conversations were common. They made the journey together, and the journey made them closer, more committed, and cohesive.

Emotion is a key word. High-performance teamwork is always an emotional experience. Human beings make it emotional, because that is part of being human. Humans want to feel a sense of team—an emotional link that warms the heart or makes it beat a little faster. They want to feel connected to something greater than themselves. They want to create, share, and grow trust in themselves, their teammates, and their leaders.

All too often, however, virtual teams lack "team" emotion—a sense of team. For example, the work that the eTeam did in this chapter's opening story was unprecedented. The young eTeam had moved mountains—turning out new services and finding new revenue sources each month that were measured in millions of dollars. Amazing! Yet the leaders failed to use the all hands meeting to build team emotion virtually to celebrate, drive, and continue their phenomenal success.

> High-performance teamwork is always an emotional experience. Human beings make it emotional, because that is part of being human.

The leaders in the opening story made the mistake of thinking that the people in their virtual organization wanted to hear about numbers and projections. Although numbers and projections are important for some team meetings, I have yet to see any team at a celebration ceremony mulling over their project plan or making boring speeches about financial forecasts. Quite the contrary, people talk about the excitement of breaking through barriers, sharing heartfelt comments from customers, and tales of beating the odds together. It's a time for stories. It's time for smiles. For some teams, it's also time to prepare for the next milestone.

> All too often, however, virtual teams lack "team" emotion—a sense of team.

Why is it that when a team meets via a conference call or other virtual media, eLeaders miss this incredibly powerful time to generate sense of team? Is it because they are stuck in the Disabled and Mechanical Phases, accepting of boring, mind-numbing business conference calls? Is it that they don't think they can be inspiring and motivational from afar?

Breaking out of the Disabled and Mechanical Phases may seem risky and uncomfortable to some eLeaders. After all, who hasn't heard a joke over a conference call that yielded no audible response from distant locations. If you have that fear, remember Chuck Yeager's risk. Several pilots had died trying to break the sound barrier. The faster he sped toward Mach 1, the more unstable his plane felt. As the plane encountered more turbulence, he took a different course than the unsuccessful pilots. He slammed the throttle forward and literally burst through the previously impenetrable barrier. eLeaders, it is time to slam the throttle forward and become Bionic.

Bionic eLeaders know that a motivated team will outperform an unmotivated one, every time. They know that communicating in ways that keep people in high spirits is time well invested. As a result, they have an unwavering commitment to build sense of team across all locations.

To Bionic eLeaders, distance isn't a barrier. Instead, technology creates the bridge, acting like an amplifier to reach every location with messages that create a fast, cohesive team that just happens to work all over the world.

To Bionic eLeaders, distance isn't a barrier. Instead, technology creates the bridge, acting like an amplifier to reach every location with messages that create a fast, cohesive team that just happens to work all over the world.

Sense of team is about stories— not just any story, but the ones that are designed to deliver the communication eTeams seek and need for future success. It's stories that make people feel included and feel good about their contribution. It's stories of people who went the extra mile to serve customers or get the product out ahead of the competition. It's stories that build excitement about the future, helping everyone know how they can make the team more successful with the challenges ahead.

eMotion: The Key to Building Sense of Team

When you hear people say, "We have too much information and not enough communication," they are asking you for eMotion.

eMotion is deliberately spelled with a small *e,* like e-mail and e-commerce. It is designed to help leaders deliver the communication messages your people want, from afar.

- The prefix *e* in eMotion stands for *electronic,* or virtual, because eLeaders will use media to communicate the message that builds sense of team. Whether leaders use conference calls, video conferences, Web conferences, studio broadcasts, or streamed audio or video events (digitally recorded and played back over the Internet)—the sense of team message is delivered virtually, not face to face. Choosing the right media for your sense of team message is key.

- The *Motion* part of eMotion represents *forward movement,* because progress, completion, and the journey build sense of team. Stories are hidden in remote pockets that speak to courage, dedication, and improved success. These stories will help people feel and celebrate sense of team, without being physically present to see it firsthand. Likewise, the stories that shape team attitudes and prepare everyone at every location for success in the journey ahead also build sense of team.

- The entire word eMotion is about our humanness as it relates to sense of team, *virtually.* People want to feel— and be—connected. eMotion is about creating sense of team when people are not in one place. Communication that builds eMotion is designed to make people feel connected to something worthwhile and to celebrate the attitudes and teamwork that breed success across all sites.

Let's look at the ways some Bionic eLeaders built eMotion and high performance in their dispersed eTeams.

Create eMotion about the Team's Work

If you think you have a problem leading inspirational eMeetings with your team, consider Chuck Roberts's challenge.

Roberts is a manager at IBM. He is leading the development effort for the Kaiser Permanente Rocky Mountain Region Clinical Information System. Now if, while holding back a great big yawn, you are wondering how anything about creating an information system can be inspiring, so was I. Somehow, writing millions of lines of code sounds about as exciting as running a marathon with a bowling ball chained to my feet—exhausting and painful!

Roberts said, "I had to create an enriching, encouraging environment for people to feel passionate about what they were doing." With people split in different locations across the Rocky Mountain Region, his challenge was great. Part of the team worked for Kaiser Permanente, and the other worked for IBM. He had to create a motivating session that inspired people from different worlds: medical doctors and software experts.

Like leaders in many other technical organizations, Roberts was also very concerned to attract and retain highly skilled people. Salaries were at an all time high. Roberts knew it would take more than large salaries and benefits to keep his people from wanting to go elsewhere. Part of his solution was deliberately to create eMotion about the team and the team's important work.

Roberts succeeded because he did not frame his monthly meetings around technical requirements and status reports. Instead, he framed the meetings as a key way to enhance the partnership between IBM and Kaiser. The partnership's mission was to change the course of health care, to improve it in ways that had been only a dream in the past. He focused his all hands meetings on the very human face of their work. Their team's work saved lives, increased safety, and acted as a beacon to improve patient care. People left that monthly meeting feeling inspired—as individuals and as a global team—because Roberts purposefully created eMotion about their work.

At the eMeeting, Roberts made it a point to include doctors from Kaiser. The doctors were not there to talk about their technical specialty. Instead, their role was to create eMotion by telling stories about the human impact of their system. One of the doctors told a story about a woman who was involved in a serious car accident that very week. Her life was saved because of the information system IBM and Kaiser had developed and installed just a few weeks earlier.

> Their role was to create eMotion by telling stories about the human impact of their system.

If any of us are in an accident and are taken to the hospital emergency room, the doctors and nurses have to act quickly. If you are lucky, you'll make it to the emergency room with your driver's license and little else. Health care workers may have to make split second decisions about how to help you, without any knowledge of your medical history, allergies, medications, or other records. If the Emergency Room team administers a drug to which you are allergic, that lack of knowledge could cost you your life.

With the system that Kaiser and IBM partnered to develop, if the patient was at a Kaiser hospital, all of those records would be available online in seconds, with allergies and critical information (like diabetes) quickly visible up front. The information system this team created saved a woman's life. That's eMotion!

> The human stories make the mandate for the technology real.

According to a report issued by the Institute of Medicine, up to 98,000 people die in hospitals each year because of medication "system errors." A system error might be from poor penmanship from doctors (surprise!) or determining the written dosage (e.g., milligrams versus micrograms). A pharmacist could misread dramatically different drugs that have similar names, like Celebrex (a pain killer) and Cerebyx (an antiseizure medication).

For decades, medicine has been searching for a solution to eliminate system errors like these. Roberts's team is finally delivering it—and more. The human stories make the mandate for the technology real. It gives people a greater purpose than just writing code. That's eMotion!

In other eMeetings, Roberts routinely creates eMotion by involving people who have stories and perspectives to build up the team, create a unified culture, and inspire pride. One IBM executive, for example, had worked on the Space Shuttle program. Now, most of us are amazed by the awesome achievements of the space program, as well as the statement its success makes about the innovativeness of humanity. In the eMeeting, the IBM executive didn't give facts and figures about growth and projections. Instead, he created eMotion by relating why he felt the Kaiser-IBM project was as important as the space program. The work the team created in this partnership would change the face of medicine as we know it, and would touch every life. That's eMotion!

The IBM-Kaiser Information System team won the 1999 Davies Award as the "best electronic retrieval system in 1999." Because of their success in their Colorado pilot, they are currently expanding the program nationwide, and then to other places in the world.

Celebrate Forward eMotion

Success breeds success. In eTeams, people can't see successes unless someone thinks to share it and celebrate it across locations. Bionic eLeaders are meticulous in finding and amplifying stories that help people in all locations sense the eTeam's forward movement. One kind of forward motion is that which has already happened. If forward motion has a metric, the metric is delivered briefly in ways that illustrate the leap, then backed up with stories about a person or team that acted heroically in making that number climb. Their heroic best practices, attitudes, and lessons learned—all of these create a foundation for the legend from which great eTeams are built.

Take one leader of a corporate university of a major long-distance and cell phone service provider. With 180 trainers around the world but dwindling resources, the team decided to hold the annual meeting virtually, rather than face to face. Because everyone on this team knew many people who had lost their jobs to reengineering, the company culture to save costs and save jobs was very strong. They still had a lot of anxiety, however, about losing the option to travel to this all-important annual event. Being face to face, in one location, for three days had been the norm for years. The annual meeting in face-to-face format was considered an important benefit.

Rather than traveling, this team held a four-hour Tele-Round Table video conference meeting (split in half with a two-hour lunch break in the middle). In most cases, four hours of video conference is too long. Not so with this Tele-Round Table meeting. Built on the metaphor of King Arthur (from my last book), the meeting was designed to create eMotion.

Olde English style trumpeters heralded the start of the eMeeting. The first half hour was spent viewing, celebrating, and recapping the many successes the eTeam had created over the past year. Customer successes. Team successes. New curriculum successes. Cross location collaboration successes. Regional successes. Metric successes. New program successes.

Importantly, the leaders were not all located at one spot. To the contrary, one key leader, plus other special guests, was at each main video site. Rotating sites, the leaders created positive eMotion about the past year's successes. They energized the message with an array of cues that drove the participants to many rounds of spontaneous applause and celebration.

> *Bionic eLeaders are meticulous in finding and amplifying stories that help people in all locations sense the eTeam's forward movement.*

Another 15 minutes were spent creating eMotion around the celebrations that were to occur later that day, across the many time zones. Building eMotion from the metaphor of King Arthur, the team leader said, "At the conclusion of our meeting at the Tele-Round Table, a Royal coach (in the form of a charter bus) will pick up you and your fellow knights at the front door of your building . . . . In Chicago it will transport you to the elegant (name of restaurant), where the royal chef and royal host will greet you. You will be escorted to . . ." The description of the restaurant in each key city and the celebration and honors that would continue were delivered with excitement and received with excitement.

From my location in Atlanta (not the headquarters), I saw people break out in spontaneous applause, smiles, and enthusiasm constantly throughout the Tele-Round Table meeting. No one was inattentive. No one left the room. They felt genuine excitement about a year that was worth being excited about. People didn't have to be in one room to feel it. From the camera angles, we could see the same happen in Illinois and New Jersey, as their celebration bridged the distance.

> The eLeader was a dynamic and moving speaker, framing every issue in a very personal way, so that people felt the message in their hearts.

Another eMotional part of the Tele-Round Table meeting was when one of their major customers talked about what it was like to be a customer of this organization. The customer's presentation reinforced the progress the eTeam had made in one year's time, and set the tone for success for the next year. The customer was well rehearsed, but came across as very genuine, as did all of the other leaders at the Tele-Round Table event.

After a break, the eLeader set the tone for the next year. She helped everyone understand the new direction, the new priorities, and the new ways the team was to work to be successful. She was a dynamic and moving speaker, framing every issue in a very personal way, so that people felt the message in their hearts.

This meeting was a success because the Tele-Round Table eTeam planned eMotion into the event. People need to celebrate, and people don't have to be in one room to do that. This was one of the most successful meetings this organization had ever had, including the face-to-face ones from previous years.

Prepare for Future eMotion

If you want your eTeam or eOrganization to move forward fast, everyone needs to be InTouch with the eMotion of creating success in the weeks and months ahead.

Does your eTeam span more than eight time zones? Does your eTeam have mobile team members who have to attend to urgent customer issues and can't break away to attend an eMeeting? If so, then you know the loss when some people never hear key messages or participate in eMeetings that are designed to create and mobilize team eMotion.

If you want your eTeam or eOrganization to move forward fast, everyone needs to be InTouch with the eMotion of creating success in the weeks and months ahead.

Dr. Eric Schmidt, CEO of Novell, hosts a quarterly audio report that is designed specifically for all employees at Novell. Even though this program is not presented live, it has a dynamic format that creates eMotion around key initiatives. The half-hour program is streamed (digitally recorded) so that employees around the world can link to it anytime, anywhere, through their network. All employees have to do is click on a button on Novell's Intranet.

The purpose of Novell's Quarterly Report is to generate momentum around a key initiative. Dr. Schmidt is an engaging eSpeaker who is highly skilled in communicating via an array of technologies. He opens the Quarterly Report with a key theme and some insights. For most of the report, however, he interviews key people whose perspectives and input underscore the eMeeting theme.

In one Quarterly Report, for example, he built eMotion around the Novell Directory Service, a crown jewel product for Novell. After Dr. Schmidt's opening remarks, he interviewed a representative from Dallas, a technician in Utah, and an executive in New Jersey. All were working on different projects but were linked into the same initiative. The interviews were a lively exchange between Schmidt and the relevant guests. By the end of the report, employees around the world had the same clear understanding of the importance of the Novell Directory Service, as well as how each could participate in making that initiative successful.

Another Quarterly Report came from the field from the CEO. This streamed audio event summarized where the CEO had traveled. Schmidt relayed what customers were saying about doing business with Novell. The report outlined key events that were important for everyone to know. Schmidt used the Quarterly Report to create eMotion about the challenges for the company down the line, as well as to let employees know what they should focus on.

> *Messages with eMotion don't require professional speech writers and public relations experts. They are simple and genuine and delivered from the heart.*

Novell's Quarterly Report is successful not because Schmidt presents information. Instead Schmidt and the guests communicate. The eAudience doesn't listen to the Quarterly Report to get a break from their daily grind. Instead, they listen because it creates eMotion about the initiative. Underscoring a theme, Schmidt and guests communicate context, stories, and perspectives that make this initiative relevant to the employees' and the company's success. The topics are so carefully chosen, and this eMeeting so well delivered, that listening to it is officially considered "an appropriate use of time during the workday."

eMotion Is Very Personal

Messages with eMotion don't require professional speech writers and public relations experts. They are simple and genuine and delivered from the heart. They are deliberately designed to touch other hearts so the team feels like a team and reinforces its connection.

Take Jerry Pederson, VP of Financial Services Solutions at Compaq Computers. He said, "As the world gets increasingly complex and our products get more complex, many leaders lose sight about keeping leadership messages simple and consistent." He was speaking about his experience as Senior VP of Sales and Service at Tandem. Although Tandem is now a part of Compaq, the Tandem culture still runs strong in their new organization.

> *The focus is to showcase people taking heroic action, showing heroic attitudes, and creating heroic results with customers.*

One simple message that was key to Tandem's success was Nonstop. Nonstop is a word that appeared on their mainframes, with good reason. Nonstop wasn't just a marketing word or label. Pederson said, "The whole company had Nonstop about it. No one put a Tandem computer in unless they had to have the mainframe running all the time, Nonstop. If it wasn't running, we had to move heaven and earth to get that customer back online."

To create a culture that was truly Nonstop, the leaders needed more than a word and a great technical machine. How did they do it? The leaders had to instill a deep Nonstop culture that literally circled the world. The leaders did that by making Nonstop very human and very personal with every Tandem employee. In the early days, when the company was new, customers had a choice: the well-established Big Blue (IBM), or the startup with spirit (Tandem). Buying from the "new kid on the block" was a bigger risk.

The leaders were successful in driving fast, cohesive eTeamwork by making Nonstop personal. Pederson said, "Everyone in the company knew that every CIO who made a decision for us put his career in our hands." Leaders transformed Nonstop (a technical descriptor of their equipment) into an eMotional message (a human descriptor of the team). Simple, consistent emphasis on the human side of Nonstop transformed 10,000 people into a single team of people who cared worldwide.

The leaders delivered the Nonstop message via technology in ways that touched everyone—sales, service, manufacturing, marketing, and every other function. Stories showed the company heroes—the people, the teams, the attitudes that built a great company. Nonstop was one of several key themes that generated eMotion by the way the eLeaders led results from afar. eMotion galvanized a level of entrepreneurship that was the envy of Silicon Valley and the world.

eMotion Is about the Hero's Journey More Than the Hero

Virtual events that are designed to build sense of team shouldn't look or feel like an Academy Awards show. Instead, the event is better described as a celebration of heroic actions that exemplify actions for all. The focus is to showcase people taking heroic action, showing heroic attitudes, and creating heroic results with customers. These stories build a legend while creating fast, cohesive eTeamwork.

From isolated, "remote" locations, people can't see the legend. Stories with eMotion help everyone in every location see the legend that people around the world are building. Stories showcase how people are collaborating successfully across distance, how people have pulled off miracles virtually, and how people are working with heartfelt commitment in serving customers. The session is filled with learning, insights, and wonderful nuggets that bond people. Bionic eLeaders seek these stories, then amplify them in ways that build sense of team.

The bottom line is that stories with eMotion make people feel good, increase their sense of connection, and amplify a culture for success that everyone knows and participates in. *The more these events are linked with the team's Moments of Truth, the greater the impact and the greater the bonding.*

B I O N I C

eTeamwork Checklist

eMotion: Building Sense of Team, from Afar

This chapter began with the quote: "Leaders can't create connectedness. Rather, believe that it is already there. Then look for ways to facilitate that connectedness."

In the Disabled and Mechanical Phases of eTeamwork, communication that builds sense of team is reserved for a face-to-face visit, if it happens at all. In between those one-site meetings, people exchange heavy doses of e-mail, voice mail, and boring conversations that usually strip away most, if not all, of the message's humanity.

Bionic eLeaders know that building sense of team is a critical component for success. Sense of team isn't about information. It's about enhancing team eMotion in ways that inspire individuals, the team, and teamwork, from afar. Messages with eMotion create and enhance sense of team. They include communication that bonds people, makes them feel happy, and makes everyone feel a part of the important work the team is doing. Messages with eMotion celebrate forward motion and prepare people for future motion as well. Importantly, eMotion is not about hype, but rather is authentic, warm communication whose purpose is to build sense of team and enhance eTeamwork. Bionic eLeaders deliberately create eMotion around being a great team that doesn't need to be in one place to be fast and cohesive.

Bionic eLeaders build eMotion virtually, by focusing not on relaying information, but instead on communicating the message in ways that foster team attitudes, team pride, and team excellence:

❏ *Don't just share information about improved team metrics. Instead, create eMotion about the metrics.* Communicate the human story (the challenge, the dedication, the attitudes) that built the dramatic rise in results.

❐ *Don't just say "Great job, team." Instead create eMotion about being a part of the team.* Communicate the human story about how the team's work touched lives, how people worked well together through technology, how people overcame obstacles, and how customers perceived their interaction with the team.

❐ *Don't just share information about the new focus or direction. Instead, create eMotion about it.* Communicate to shape attitudes about it, provide resources, and respond to issues.

❐ *Don't just talk about customers or products. Instead, create eMotion about your customers and products.* Link customers, experts, and key players into the online team meeting. Make sure people interact, not sit silent, during the session.

❐ *Don't shy away from negative news. Instead, create eMotion for the team to learn from it or work better together.* Communicate to define and refine the solution so everyone interacts, learns, and knows how to handle the situation better as a team.

THINGS YOU CAN DO TODAY TO
Build Sense of Team from Afar

eLeaders	eTeams	Individuals
Create a plan for how you will build sense of team from afar. • Become very disciplined about discovering and building sense of team. • Deliver sense of team messages often, on a schedule, in a location-neutral format. • Build the message around the journey and the lessons learned in the journey. • Deliver the messages in a warm, personal way through technology appropriate for your eTeam.	Create a plan to increase sense of team from afar. • Establish a plan to gather and amplify sense of team messages. • Take responsibility to share good news that only you can see at your site, but that makes others on the team feel good about being a part of the team. • Contribute ways to share successes and best practices that make people feel good. • Begin every team eMeeting with eMotion.	Take the time to make sure people feel good about communicating with you from afar. • Amplify good news that only you can see at your site to people that may benefit from the sense of team message. • Consciously work at building sense of team in all of the communication you send virtually. • Use eMeeting technology in ways that build high-level, quality interaction. • Take the time to relate sense of team messages with people you communicate with routinely, from afar.

8

Building Team eMotion through Media

> It is not enough to have the best talent. You must have the best team.
> **Dan Rather**
> MSNBC, October 20, 2000

The sales organization for a company that produces industrial gasses (such as oxygen) surpassed their revenue projections. Their success was not due to an expanding marketplace. Actually, in their market, the competitive environment was the most challenging in its history. Small start-up companies, offering lower pricing, posed a significant threat in the company's key markets across the United States. Yet, this sales team pulled its act together, shared their best practices, and exceeded the company's ambitious revenue target.

Their success wasn't because of extraordinary sales from one or two people. Instead, every salesperson pulled her weight from whichever state they were based. Expectations for the year were high. By the year's end, every sales representative had exceeded them. The team received special honors at the all-day President's meeting at corporate headquarters. Speaking from the auditorium stage at the firm's annual event, the President praised the sales team. He spoke for several minutes, going into detail about how the team broke through to meet their challenge. Truly this team was a new model for the company. They had learned to work well virtually—something more teams would be doing in the months ahead. At the end of the glowing testimonial, the President presented the eLeader with a trophy. The audience broke out in spontaneous applause, then stood up in a rousing standing ovation.

> *Unfortunately, because of distance, only 3 of the team's 15 members were able to participate in the ceremony.*

Unfortunately, because of distance, only 3 of the team's 15 members were able to participate in the ceremony. Each of the 3 worked within an hour's drive from headquarters, and therefore made the short commute to take part in the event. The other 12 would have had to fly in for the event. The eLeader had no budget to cover their travel. As a result, each of the 12 "pounded the pavement" like every other normal day, fully excluded from the ceremony and camaraderie of their teammates.

> *The ceremony stirred a lot of eMotion in this dispersed team: exclusion, isolation, and aloneness.*

At the end of the ceremony, the eLeader sent an e-mail to the 12, briefly describing the event. One of the 12 sloughed off his disappointment, then described how he felt. "It reminded me of a T-shirt I saw on vacation recently. The T-shirt said, 'My parents spent their vacation in Maui, and all I got was this lousy T-shirt.'" After all the hard work, he felt left out of the fun and recognition. The ceremony stirred a lot of eMotion in this dispersed team. For the 12, however, it was not the eMotion that any leader wants: exclusion, isolation, and aloneness.

This company had been globally dispersed for years, yet they held ceremonies like this that clearly showed they weren't really global in the way they communicated. Before the awards ceremony, no one at HQ thought to link in a live audio or video connection so that others in the organization, particularly the distant sales team members, could participate. No one thought to record that part of the awards ceremony for playback on the sales eTeam's Web site. No one thought to use media (like voice mail) to share the President's personal congratulations with *every* member of the Sales eTeam, not just those who were able to travel to the event.

This organization is clearly stuck in the Disabled Phase. People had to be physically present to participate in the ceremony. If we look at the event itself from an HQ perspective, it appears successful. If we look at it from afar, however, the very nature of the event broke down sense of team. Why, even the trophy reflected this organization's locationcentric bias. It was not enough that most of the team were excluded from the ceremony. Most were also excluded from ever seeing the trophy, which would reside in some distant office the team members would never visit. Old methods don't work in a new model: the truly global corporation.

Virtual teams are hungry for the warmth and glue that sense of team messages create. Bionic eLeaders choose to communicate their sense of team messages in ways that everyone feels—and is—included. To them, technology is not the solution. Instead, media is the conduit that enables everyone in every location to bask in the messages that create sunshine, generate warmth, and give life to the team's spirit.

> *Virtual teams are hungry for the warmth and glue that sense of team messages create.*

Right Media for Sense of Team Message

Bionic eLeaders know that they have a world of media choices for communication with their eTeam. They embrace media as an extension of their ability to communicate on a personal level with people anywhere.

Whether you lead a team of 5 or 10,000, you have an exciting array of media choices to amplify your all-important sense of team message to everyone on the team, no matter where in the world they reside. In fact, the power of hardware, software, and networks on our desktops today rival the capability of million-dollar radio and TV studios, as well as the elaborate video teleconference rooms of only a decade ago. From our desktops, we can connect via a live video or Web conference and stream (digitally record) it. In a flash, we can survey audience participants with live online polling and interactive audience dialogue. We can create a slide presentation, attach an audio file, and design it for kiosk-type playback from your desktop. Still others create elaborate CD-ROMs, with slick backgrounds, fancy graphics, and music fades.

Importantly, the technology is not what builds sense of team. Sense of team is a very personal, human event. Media, used well, lets everyone be a part of the sense of team eCommunication moments, never disadvantaged by location.

If you've ever suffered through someone's boring home movies or horrid virtual presentation, though, you know that media does not an expert make. Communicating through media is an art. For Bionic eLeaders, it's about *connecting* with an audience that you can't see, and that may not be able to see you (depending on the media you choose). Media requires skills that don't happen naturally, but are critical for "the human connection" to occur.

> *Media, used well, lets everyone be a part of the sense of team eCommunication moments, never disadvantaged by location.*

Making a human connection through media is a key success factor for all eLeaders in the new millennium.

Suddenly, it's no longer enough for eLeaders and eTeams to know how to create rapport. The next evolution is to master how to create rapport without travel, without ever shaking someone's hand. Sound impossible? It's not. With the right media and the right message, it's very possible. For Bionic eLeaders and Bionic eTeams, it happens all the time.

If people aren't going to be in one place, then they have to communicate through some technology. With so many alternatives, many eLeaders and eTeams wonder, "What is the right media for the message?" They are looking for a simple formula that will ensure that their message is received well by people whose faces they can't see.

The answer to the question is not simple. No matrix works for all sense of team messages because too many variables come into play. Picture in your mind the many virtual teams in your world. When you look a little closer, you'll see:

- *The distribution of eTeam members is different.* Some teams are split across two locations; others, across hundreds.

- *The eLeader's ability to create a warm, personal presence through media is different.* Some leaders have excellent communication skills; others struggle, especially through media.

- *The media choices are different.* Some eTeams are skilled in wide array of technologies. Others don't even know which technologies exist.

- *The ways to get feedback are different.* Some have robust tools that allow fast, live interaction; others enable only slow feedback.

- And many more.

This chapter focuses on key variables that will help you make better media choices for your sense of team communication. As Bionic eLeader Anthony Robbins of SGI says, "There aren't many things people can't do in a distributed environment if leaders are open to new ways and new opportunities to lead and communicate." Right on!

Select Location-Neutral Media and Delivery

The first step in creating sense of team through media is to relay your message in a location-neutral way. Location neutral means that no site is disadvantaged from participating in or accessing the message firsthand.

Actions speak louder than words. Before you utter the first word of your sense of team message, the media that you choose reflects whether you really view your team as (1) *global* or (2) *local with remote locations.* The right media for your "sense of team" message always reflects the former, a global orientation.

When a team has a global orientation, everyone is first to receive the message, by the Bionic eLeader's design. Location-neutral media and delivery let every eTeam member in every location log on, access, or receive the sense of team communication at one time, worldwide. The "one time" is not always during the workday at the eLeader's location. Instead, "one time" is defined by the eTeam so that everyone feels included or disadvantaged by location, as shown in these examples:

- *Location-neutral media and delivery can be interactive.* Take one Europe-U.S. eTeam that was separated by six time zones. The people on this team knew they had only a two-hour window when people on both sides of the Atlantic were in their normal work days. They chose always to hold eMeetings to build sense of team during that two-hour window.

- *Location-neutral media and delivery can also be noninteractive.* A growing number of virtual teams span eight or more time zones. As a result, they do not have a window of time in which to connect interactively to build sense of team. In that case, the team selects location-neutral media and delivery, so that no one is excluded. Dr. Eric Schmidt, the Bionic CEO at Novell, chose the location-neutral approach. Because he identified his team as covering the globe, not just headquarters, he chose to stream (digitally record for playback through the Intranet) an audio or video sense of team session.

Match the Bionic eLeader's Communication Acumen to the Media

One of the most famous debates of the past century was broadcast simultaneously on television and radio. The debaters, John F. Kennedy and Richard M. Nixon, were the 1960 Democratic and Republican nominees for president of the United States. Surveys showed that the people who watched the debate on television felt that Kennedy won. The people who listened on the radio, however, felt that Nixon had won.

What made the difference? TV was a strong medium for Kennedy; radio was strong for Nixon. Despite the youthful age that plagued him, Kennedy created a strong, confident presence in front of the camera. As he looked into the camera's eye, he skillfully connected with the viewing audience. Kennedy looked calm, cool, and collected. That same camera's eye showed Nixon with beads of sweat above his lips. During the debates, Nixon appeared nervous and tense when viewed through the camera's eye. The radio listeners, however, couldn't see Nixon's tension. They did hear his words, his thoughts, and his policies, which came across better than Kennedy's through the radio.

Whether your team has 10 or 10,000 members, communicating humanly through media is a key skill for eLeaders. It is not enough to be a strong communicator in one medium, or even one of each type (one interactive and one noninteractive). Bionic eLeaders actively grow their human ability to connect with distant people on a human level through multiple media.

> Bionic eLeaders actively grow their human ability to connect with distant people on a human level through multiple media.

If you've ever been embarrassed by the way you come across in a photo, shocked by the way you sound through a recorder, or offended by the mannerisms of some spin doctor on the news analysis programs—you know that communicating through media is different than face to face. Technology changes the texture and feel of the communication—that is, until people get more skilled at communicating through media.

Skill doesn't mean that eLeaders and eTeams get "slick" in portraying an image, like an award-winning actor on a stage or a highly polished anchor on the nightly news. Instead, skill is about mastering how to make an authentic human connection through media. The eLeader's skills must flourish through the media, establishing a virtual presence that is genuine, relaxed, and personal. Without the human connection, the impact from the sense of team event will be dramatically lessened.

What if an eLeader's ability is stronger in e-mail or written media? Isn't that enough? For today, perhaps. For tomorrow, however, it's not fast, powerful, and interactive enough. When traditional teams build sense of team, they don't sit down and type messages to one another. They dedicate a few moments of their time to be together, interact, and talk. When teams work virtually, they need to dedicate that same interactive time to interact and feel like a team. That's the key reason why eLeaders must master how to create human connections through audio, video, studio, and Web media. Everyone's skills can be improved, and it can really be a lot of fun!

Set an Effective eAtmosphere to Build Sense of Team

Do you remember which United States president was famous for his "Fireside Chats"? The answer is Franklin Delano Roosevelt. Elected in the early 1930s, he took office in the depths of the Great Depression, where up to one-third of the U.S. population was out of work. FDR had to lead the country through bank failures, the stock market crash, and World War II. Truly, these years were among the nation's—and the world's—darkest hours, threatening the people, the nation itself, and people from other countries of the world.

Roosevelt was a Bionic eLeader, even back in his day, because he used technology (the radio) to pull citizens together and lead them through these difficult years. Now, he could have gone on the radio and read a boring speech. But that was not the atmosphere he wanted to create. He wanted a warm and close feeling with each citizen listener, like a family gathering around a fireplace to talk with him informally.

Fireside Chats was the metaphor that set the tone for sessions that were purposefully designed to extend Roosevelt's human touch. The sessions created a personal connection from the listeners to him, to each other, and to their great nation. Throughout this powerful metaphor, Roosevelt transformed a splintering nation into a "team" that stretched from the Atlantic to the Pacific, and to points all over the world. Roosevelt created a sense of community through the radio that brought out the best in people.

> *Roosevelt was a Bionic eLeader because he used technology (the radio) to pull citizens together and lead them through these difficult years.*

When one looks at the Fireside Chats from dispersed locations, the metaphor creates interesting images of the time. Historic pictures show families gathered around their home's oversized radio to listen to Roosevelt. In those days, radios stood about as tall as the top of a computer monitor on a modern desk today. People huddled their chairs in a circle around the gigantic wooden radio box, as if the technology were another person in the circle.

In actuality, the room where Roosevelt made his Fireside Chats had no fireplace at all. He did the broadcasts from a small, barren chamber in the basement of the White House. Fireside Chat was a metaphor he used to create a warm environment to talk with citizens and bring out their best.

With today's media, eLeaders have limitless opportunity to create an equally profound effect through media. Depending on the size of a team (10, 10,000, or more) and the resources (no staff or a multiperson dedicated staff), Bionic eLeaders build sense of team through a host of video, audio, and streaming technologies. Then, using a metaphor or theme, Bionic eLeaders turn conference calls into live radio talk shows. Some create their own version of a Fireside Chat. Other Bionic eLeaders transform video or Web meetings into live TV talk shows. They use popular commercial program formats, such as Oprah, Larry King, or Politically Incorrect.

> *The metaphor of the talk show or themed event focuses everyone on the event, not the technology.*

Importantly, the metaphor of the talk show or themed event focuses everyone on the event, not the technology. The result is that the focus is on the message and the human connection. Most of the previous examples can be done with few resources.

Some companies, however, spend significant resources on building sense of team globally. At the head of the line is First Friday, a video program that Tandem used to align all 10,000 of its employees around the world on growth objectives. The focus of First Friday was to build eMotion around strategy and direction, so that everyone knew what everyone in the company had to know to be successful.

First Friday was a one-hour monthly program. The eAtmosphere was a mix of the humorous skits of Saturday Night Live, the playful yet meaty interaction on Politically Incorrect, and fast clips from the field like on MSNBC—all featuring Tandem employees and customers. First Friday featured the corporation's top leaders, who interacted with the audience and studio guests in an informal, conversational, and sometimes playful manner. First Friday also included special guests from other parts of the company, as well as customers and experts.

Each month's eMeeting telecast focused on a single theme, like customer satisfaction or targeted growth opportunities. Although the telecast was engaging and entertaining, none of its content was fluff. Minisegments were pieced together skillfully to engage the audience and build sense of team that spanned the world.

First Friday was brilliant. It created sense of team worldwide with leaner management than other companies dream of. Not every team needs an event this elaborate to build sense of team. But every team does need an effective sense of team event that matches their technology and their team.

The greatest danger every eLeader faces is to make your sense of team event feel like yet another business presentation. Technology doesn't create the human connection. The leader must do that. The metaphor or theme guides the event to create the right atmosphere, virtually.

Rehearse until It Sounds and Feels Unrehearsed

With the pace of work today, people want to build sense of team, but they want the eSession to be fast, focused, and fun. Bionic eLeaders carefully structure sense of team sessions to take the minimal time but deliver the maximum message.

In one sense of team eMeeting, Anthony Robbins distributed ownership of the conference call among other eLeaders on his core team, who worked from other locations. He said, "We rehearsed the entire conference call to be sure we were crisp in delivery."

All of the leaders in the call wanted the meeting to feel vibrant and lively. They wanted the eParticipants to feel like they were all in one room, going around the table, even though they were going across phone lines and couldn't see each other. The leaders wanted everyone to feel—and be—included, by design. In the rehearsal, the leaders set norms, timelines, and eMotion messages for the maximum human impact.

> *Technology doesn't create the human connection.*

Build in Feedback Loops, and Make the Feedback Visible

Feedback is the breakfast of champions! If you want to build a team that feels like champions and acts like champions, build in feedback that lets you know how well you're building sense of team.

Some Bionic eLeaders ask for feedback before the first sense of team communication event. Take George Davis, cofounder and Bionic eLeader of Davis & Deane. Davis & Deane partners with and licenses trainers all over the world to deliver their phenomenally successful project management and leadership simulations.

Davis knew he wanted to have team communication whose sole purpose was to enhance human connections worldwide. Team members covered nearly every time zone around the world. Some had Internet access through high-speed lines (ISDN, DSL, T1, T3), while others still struggled with much slower modem and phone line speeds.

Rather than making the decision by himself, he asked his team for feedback about what communication they wanted from him to enhance their sense of team. Some requests were as simple as sending a photo of Davis in his office in Seattle, which he did.

All the people on the virtual team unanimously agreed on one item. Davis is a natural philosopher, and he knows how to talk philosophy in ways that engage, inspire, and challenge people to greater heights. All wanted Davis to talk philosophy as it related to the company, the customers, and people. In other words, they wanted to know what he was thinking. So, he told them.

Because of the unique time zone and technology con-straints of this team, Davis sent his sense of team communi-cation monthly via Lotus Notes. Importantly, he wrote it like a "fireside chat," not like a report or news article. Through this team communication, he revealed something of himself. He reiterated the values that bind the organization and build it into a successful worldwide team their customers love. This sense of team Notes Event is noninteractive, yet it creates a per-sonal moment that works well in the team. Davis knows that, because he gets feedback constantly.

Few Bionic eLeaders have the time and talent to write as creatively and powerfully as Davis. With today's technology alternatives, Bionic eLeaders have a whole new array of eMeeting options: interactive Web conferencing, video streaming, audio streaming with still pictures, and more. Bionic eLeaders and Bionic eTeams have to learn which choices work best. The best way to learn which message and which technologies work for your sense of team eMeeting is through feedback. You'll need lots of feedback, on many levels — before, during, and after the sense of team eMeeting. You'll also need a strong commitment to stay the course and learn to get better. Most leaders say that feedback helps them fine tune their eMeetings until they work for their team.

Before the first event, get feedback from all (or a representative group of) the people who will participate. What communication do eTeam members want? What communication do they not want? Who should lead the eMeeting, and when should eLeadership be shared?

During a live sense of team eMeeting, get feedback at least every five minutes. Building in feedback will be the toughest part of the eMeeting, but the most important. Feedback must be relevant to the topic and the group. It needs to feel spontaneous and be spontaneous.

> *The best way to learn which message and which technologies work for your sense of team eMeeting is through feedback.*

End the sense of team eMeeting with feedback as well. Through Web conference technology, rate the eMeeting, capture comments, build a success screen, encourage verbal comments, and give rewards. Or take everyone's browsers to a feedback form. Then make sure that at least one of the comments is discussed and acted upon by the next sense of team eMeeting— or, better yet, right away.

B I O N I C

eTeamwork Checklist

How to Build eMotion, from Afar

This chapter began with a quote: "It is not enough to have the best talent. You must have the best team."

Working globally, no team can afford to wait until the next onsite meeting to build momentum and sense of team.

To be successful, every eLeader must master the new basics of how to use media to extend his personal touch. Bionic eLeaders deliberately create eMotion by selecting the right media for the sense of team moment. No quick and easy formula exists to determine the right media for the message, because there are too many variables. Bionic eLeaders make the best selection based on these criteria.

☐ Select location-neutral media and delivery.

☐ Match the Bionic eLeader's communication acumen to the media.

☐ Build sense of team through an eMeeting metaphor or theme.

☐ Rehearse until the communication sounds and feels unrehearsed.

☐ Build in feedback loops, and make them visible.

THINGS YOU CAN DO TODAY TO
Build eMotion through Media

eLeaders	eTeams	Individuals
In earnest, improve your skills and best practices for communicating through several kinds of media.	Improve your skills and best practices for communicating sense of team messages through several media.	Improve your skills and best practices in selecting media that lets you create a teamlike environment when you communicate with distant others.

eLeaders

- Choose a metaphor that works for your sense of team communication.
- Create feedback mechanisms to know that you come across as authentic, virtually.
- Add a personal touch to every sense of team event. Refer to people by name, and say thank you.
- Involve as many people as you can in conveying your sense of team messages.
- Rehearse!

eTeams

- Get very clear about the kind of communication your eTeam wants to help them create and grow sense of team.
- Create a plan for sense of team communication. Make sure that plan keeps a steady stream of sense of team communication flowing, across multiple formats.

Individuals

- Decide which media is most powerful in creating a warmer space for communication.
- When you use the media, make the session as interactive as possible.

9

The Bionics of Engaging eMeetings

> People vote with their mouse. They will log on to a meeting if it is meaningful or worthwhile. They will log off if it is not.
> **John Manzo**
> 3Com

very company has a story in its eMeeting folklore that we can identify with. Take one information technology group that meets by video teleconference once a week. To keep communication flowing, the group places the video-conference cameras in voice-activated mode. When somebody talks, the camera at their location automatically turns on. In a flash, all of the people in the other sites can see who's talking.

People who use the voice-activated mode know that any loud sound will cause the camera to switch. If you cough, sneeze, or put a coffee cup down, the camera will switch to your site. Suddenly, much to your embarrassment, you're on camera! Everyone in the other sites is looking at you, as you are caught unaware. To eliminate this problem, this eTeam established a norm about using the mute button: if you're not talking in the video teleconference, put your speaker on mute.

One day, in the middle of a video conference meeting, one team member who was sitting in a conference room by himself, fell fast asleep. He started snoring—loudly. Then the inevitable happened. He had forgotten to put on the mute button. The camera locked in on him. In a nanosecond, all 20 of his eTeammates got a close-up view of him, deep asleep, lost in the echoes of his loud snoring. The story has become a corporate legend!

We all have eMeeting horror stories. We're in one location. Everyone else is in another. We don't know what people at the other sites are doing. We hope, however, they're not doing what we're doing—which is processing our e-mail. We all know the signs that tell us people aren't really engaged in the meeting. We hear keys clicking in the background. We ask a question and the only response is silence. When people ask, "Will you repeat that question again?" we feel uneasy, unsafe, and unconnected when we meet virtually. We blame the medium, but the problem is ours.

If you lead eMeetings, here is your competition: thousands of distractions at each person's individual desktop. Each makes demands on your time and your attention. An endless stack of e-mail to process, reports to create, calendars to update, paper mail to filter, to-do lists to conquer—and the list goes on. People walk down the hallway and stop by your desk to talk, ask you a brief question, or invite you to lunch. Someone in the hotel room next to yours has their TV blaring, or one of your children happily saunters in your home office to capture some of your attention. You're trying to balance the incessant demands of an ever faster and ever heavier workload, grabbing every spare moment to get a little more work done. You can hardly afford to waste a minute. Besides, the workshop you had last week on multitasking makes you feel guilty if you do.

Bionic eTeams have a very different experience in their eMeetings than those in the opening stories of this chapter. Keith Glennan, Director of Integration and Engineering at Logicon, a Northrop Grumman Company, says, "An eMeeting is recognized as a significant investment. If it is worth having the meeting and the people at the meeting, it is worth having everyone engaged in what is going on."

The key word is engaged. Having an agenda is no longer enough. Putting up with slow, boring meetings that don't accomplish anything is no longer enough. Using interactive time for anything that can be handled by e-mail or a team Web site is no longer enough.

> *"An eMeeting is recognized as a significant investment."*

No one has the time to waste in boring, slow, unproductive eMeetings. As Steve Cook, Chief Solutions Architect at Northrop Grumman says, "The bar on expectations about eMeetings is always going up. People are not satisfied with things today that they would have lived with six months ago." If the eMeeting fails to deliver value and interaction—fast— the problems outlined earlier in this chapter will continue to plague that team.

What is an optimal length for an eMeeting? It's about one minute shorter than the point in time when anyone in your eTeam gets bored. So the key to eMeetings is mastering the new art of how to keep people engaged. You'll need more than an agenda. You'll need new best practices and new technology. The results will amaze you.

Bionic eLeaders have mastered the new art of how to create engaging, interactive eMeetings. This chapter will overview some key best practices that can make your eMeeting spontaneous, interactive, and productive.

Right Media for the eMeeting

Did you know that 97 percent of us require collaboration to do our job? Think about that for a moment. The age of the Lone Ranger is not just dead, it is ancient history—barbaric and foreign to the teams that serve a global marketplace that changes at the speed of light. Colocated teams are quickly becoming part of that history, as well. Virtual teamwork is the only way a company can effectively serve its worldwide customer base.

We have gotten very good about collaborating when people are in one room. The challenge for eTeams is to collaborate effectively and quickly when people are not in the same room. For the past decade, eTeams have had basically three choices for collaboration. Those choices are conference calls, video conferences, and collaboration by e-mail. All of these technologies are part of the Bionic eLeader's tool kit. Collaboration by these technologies, however, tends to be stiff, unnatural, and slow.

> *If you lead eMeetings, here is your competition: thousands of distractions at each person's individual desktop.*

Today, groups have wonderful new choices that enable levels of speed and interaction that far exceed anything groups attain in a colocated traditional meeting. New technology lets groups eMeet through Web conference technology. Web conferencing lets eTeams create documents together, share applications, poll and vote spontaneously, and even surf the Web together. Used with new eMeeting best practices, eMeetings with Web conference technology are faster, more interactive, and more productive than traditional meetings.

As the vendors and services change frequently, check <www.bionicteam.com> for more information on specific technologies. For now, however, know this: high-level collaboration can occur in real time (everybody interacting at one time) or 24/7 (24 hours by 7 days—all interacting at different times). This chapter covers real-time collaboration. The next covers 24/7.

Bionic eLeaders supplement conference calls and video conferences with Web conference technology. Using new best practices, Web conference technology gives your eTeam a platform to accelerate its interaction, understanding, and results. Web conferencing enables better communication, because people can spontaneously exchange higher level visual, auditory, and feeling cues.

ROI Interactive Topics

Bionic eLeaders don't call an eMeeting to share information. Instead, they look at those rare, interactive moments as an opportunity to build teamwork and sense of team, while solving problems and accomplishing results. Effective eMeetings begin with a clear focus on using *interactive* time to *interact* fast on high-value topics. The objective is to produce the highest return for everyone from the *interaction* that occurs.

Take one Bionic sales leader at Nortel. The sales team had seven people who each worked in a separate location in the western United States. Every Monday morning, the team met for one hour via a conference call. Initially, the leader had each of the salespeople give a ten-minute status report.

Web conferencing enables better communication, because people can spontaneously exchange higher level visual, auditory, and feeling cues.

Now, all of us have been in status meetings. In fact, most of us have given status reports to others numerous times. If you were one of those seven people in that electronic meeting, when is the only time you're really attending to that meeting? It's when you have to give your report, naturally. It's when you hear your name. It doesn't take a rocket scientist to know that the rest of the time, you're probably attending something else.

The leader didn't want a team in name only—the old-style sales organization, where each sales professional was out for herself. No, he wanted a real team—people who relied on each other, helped each other, and made decisions together. He knew that if he was to be successful, he had to use the team's interactive eMeeting time better. Going over status didn't build the team or improve results. So, with their full support, he changed the way they met via conference call.

Every Friday, each of the sales professionals submitted a brief status report to him by e-mail. He compiled the e-mails into a simple one-page report, then e-mailed it to the team.

When everyone dialed in for the conference call on Monday morning, each had a copy of the e-mails in hand and had reviewed it.

> *He wanted a real team—people who relied on each other, helped each other, and made decisions together.*

The eTeam spent their one hour of eMeeting time building teamwork and improving results. They reviewed the numbers as a team, celebrated their successes, and helped each other to improve all team metrics. They didn't go over status. They talked about how to *improve* status as a team. The focus of the eMeeting was to *interact* about how to improve everyone's individual performance and the team's overall results. If one eTeam member needed more knowledge about a particular product, another offered support. If another eTeam member needed mentoring, still another stepped forward to help. They talked about their customers, trends, concerns, successes, and issues. In their eMeetings, the more they interacted as a eTeam, the more they became a team.

The sales team was so successful at generating sales and momentum that it went on to be a model for other teams in the worldwide sales organization. The team acted and operated as a team, not as individuals who share information via conference call. This leader was Bionic because he didn't just have a technical link. Instead, he used a technical link to create human connections as a team.

eCollaborate, Fast!

Everyone thinks the panacea for effective meetings is to pull everyone into one room.

Conference calls and video conference meetings—these are the traditional interactive technologies for eTeams. Both are important tools that have a role in effective eMeetings. If people can't travel, they can still communicate with one another in interactive time.

The problem, however, is that these eMeeting technologies constrict the most critical communication component that builds real teamwork: *dynamic, spontaneous interaction.* For the most part, they are designed to let only one person talk at a time. With today's focus on fast teamwork, that's often far from fast enough.

Bionic eLeaders can enhance conference calls and video conferences with powerful best practices and the features of Web conference technology. Web conference technology lets the eTeam interact on a new level, from their desktop computers. Web conference might include a common eWhiteboard, eApplications, eKeyboard chat, ePolling, and other eFeatures. Used effectively by eMeeting leaders, these common Web conference features finally let people in eMeetings interact faster, decide faster, and achieve a meeting result faster than in traditional meetings.

> *Common Web conference features finally let people in eMeetings interact faster, decide faster, and achieve a meeting result faster than in traditional meetings.*

Take Marilyn Stangle, Bionic eLeader at Lucent Technologies. Before her team became Bionic, Stangle's eTeam used to start their weekly conference call meeting by verbally polling each person on the team. One at a time, each person identified what he wanted to discuss during the team's conference call. The process took too long.

Now, supplementing the conference call with Web conference technology, Stangle's team completes the whole process in less than a minute. Everyone links by conference call and holds conferences from his or her desktop. After Stangle's opening remarks, each team member is asked to go to Net-Meeting's chat feature. At her cue, each person keys an issue she wants to discuss in the interactive eMeeting. Everyone keys one idea, then hits the enter key. Suddenly, everyone in every location sees the combined display of issues that everyone in the eTeam wants solved. The team then interacts to structure a spontaneous agenda for the eMeeting based on the issues listed.

With Stangle's best practice, did everyone participate? Yes. Did everyone see the results? Yes. Was the team spontaneous in responding to its most pressing issues? Yes. Using keyboards, the whole team talked at once to get the issues on the table for all to see. Then they used that information to interact verbally and decide jointly how to spend eMeeting time.

> *"This process leaves us more time for the meat at the meeting versus spending time on administrivia."*

Stangle states, "This process leaves us more time for the meat at the meeting versus spending time on administrivia." Stangle's approach is one of many new and innovative best practices that turn Web conference features into benefits for your team. This solution is not just moving an agenda into a virtual format. Instead, it is a whole new set of best practices and techniques to produce breakthrough speed, with fantastic interaction from multiple sites.

Be Direct about eTrust

All meeting spaces create a unique environment for trust building. Compare a face-to-face team meeting to a conference call meeting. If building trust is critical for your eTeam's success, which would you choose? Most people say a face-to-face team meeting. Face to face creates an environment rich in communication cues, which can create and boost human trust.

Few will argue that virtual meetings are not tough environments for trust building. However, a few Bionic eLeaders are lighting the way for the rest of us, proving that eTeams can build high level trust through their interaction in eMeetings.

One of these pioneers is Robert Vicek, the Bionic eLeader of a corporate university within Lockheed-Martin. Facing dwindling resources, Vicek was on a quest to stretch the company's training budget. Lockheed Martin University, of which Robert is a part, is responsible for training 120,000 people located across 110 different sites.

Before Vicek's team, the company did not have a centralized training agreement from vendors. Each site found and contracted with vendors on its own. As a result, the cost to deliver the same course could range from as low as $99 in some locations to as high as $1,400 in others—*even from the same vendor!* Vicek knew that economies of scale were not being leveraged.

The charter for Vicek's team was to centralize the purchasing of some key technical courses without physically centralizing the team, not even for a day. To do that, the team had to build, solicit, and evaluate a Request for Proposal (RFP), then award the contracts—virtually. Up to this point, no one in the history of the company had tried a project like this without colocating people *twice*—once to create the RFP, then again to evaluate it.

> *Like the elegant space vehicles their company builds, however, Vicek's eTeam launched itself boldly as a faster, effective pilot for a new way to work.*

Like the elegant space vehicles their company builds, however, Vicek's eTeam launched itself boldly as a faster, effective pilot for a new way to work.

The 11 people who worked on this team had never before met face to face, nor did they have any history of working together. With Vicek's leadership, the team completed their work in 75 percent less time than typical RFPs took. They created a result that had a positive $5 million impact on the corporation. Most important, Vicek's eTeam bonded and operated with high levels of trust, reaching every decision with 100 percent consensus. Amazingly, not one dollar was spent on travel. In fact, the team chose not to travel, but instead to use Web conference technology to facilitate team interaction and trust building.

One of the key reasons this team was successful was the way in which Vicek led the team to build trust. First, he didn't ignore the topic. He addressed trust directly, up front at the first eMeeting. Vicek said, "I threw everything out on the table—both the good and the bad. I brought out that we had a lot of conflicting priorities, but we had to work together to create the right impact down the road for the company." He was open in stating the obvious about what everyone else was feeling. He was careful to be overtly neutral and open in his words and actions. That was the beginning of the trust process.

> *Virtual teams have been pining away for a virtual equivalent of the "small meeting room down the hall."*

Second, he was very clear to state key ways he would earn their trust as the team leader. Because none of the people had worked with him before, he set clear norms of what they could expect from him as the leader. One key way was to honor the eTeam's time. For example, Vicek committed up front that no eMeeting time would be wasted. If a meeting was scheduled for half an hour, then half an hour is exactly how long it would take. He established that they would have no standing eMeetings; instead, eMeetings were scheduled only when interaction of everyone at the same time was required.

Third, he set trust expectations for the team itself. Vicek said, "Everyone plays an equal role in this process." He made sure the team established standards and rules of conduct to build team and individual trust in its new environment. Virtual teams have been pining away for a virtual equivalent of the "small meeting room down the hall." You know the one. You're at your desk. A teammate is at her desk a few steps away. You have a problem. You stop by the person's desk and ask her to go with you to the meeting room down the hall. You talk interactively, brainstorm, share drawings and diagrams, push documents back and forth, use the whiteboard, expand on each other's ideas, and collaborate on many levels. You have a wonderful, spontaneous exchange. You leave the room somehow more connected on a human level, and you leave with a tangible result.

With Web conference technology, at last eTeams can create a spontaneous, interactive eMeeting space. In an earlier chapter, you read about the Global Environment, Health, & Safety Work Process Implementation Team at Dow. The eTeam had 21 people dispersed across 12 locations. They used Web conference technology to build teamwork visually during their interactive eMeeting.

According to Heather Dixon, a member of the Implementation Team, everyone was a full participant. No one felt remote or excluded. She said, "We all owned what we created on the screen together. In addition, it focused us on optimal performance across the entire planet, not just in our little corner of the world."

Fourth, when it came to issues of trust, one discussion was not enough. Vicek opened every team eMeeting with some brief comments that trust and open dialog were both required for team success. It worked.

Make It Dynamic, Visually Building the Team

During the eMeeting, the team also dynamically created team to-do lists, issues logs, and action registers. As each item was completed, the team almost made a ceremony out of checking items off the list, dynamically, together, which grew their sense of team.

> When it came to issues of trust, one discussion was not enough.

Dixon said, "Working this way, people could see how their activities affected other people and other locations. Now, a specific change was no longer one person's problem. Instead, it was an issue that we had to resolve together as a team."

Vicek, who used similar techniques with similar success, said, "I find that most teams use only a fraction of the power of Web conference technology, such as to show slides to people at another location. This technology's real strength, however, is as a dynamic, collaborative tool." Right on.

Input eWarmth

Meeting by any technology often creates a cold, mechanical feeling. Yet people are engaged by warmer, more human places to meet. Bionic eLeaders orchestrate ways to give the

eMeeting a human face. They have the skills to bring humanity into the eMeeting.

> *Whatever the tech-nique, meetings that attend to the eWarmth of the call are more engaging to everyone. Bionic eLeaders always attend to eWarmth.*

Anthony Robbins, the SGI Bionic
eLeader whom you met earlier, has input eWarmth into his eMeetings. He
says that in his eMeetings, he has to be
"motivational, inspirational, and opti-
mistic." He draws people into the call by
using their names often. In his all-
hands meetings, people who ask a
question first state their name and location. At the beginning of Robbins's response, he connects to their personal
environment. He first shares some
good news that happened at that location recently or a story
that makes everyone feel good. He constantly reaches out with
his words, building eWarmth.

Some leaders use photos. Others use eMeetings with customers. Still others frame issues in ways that connect people
positively during the meeting. Whatever the technique, meetings that attend to the eWarmth of the call are more engaging
to everyone. Bionic eLeaders always attend to eWarmth.

Russell Kern is President of Kern Direct Marketing, a
direct marketing advertising agency. The firm's specialty is
generating sales leads for leading edge technology companies. Meeting first with customers via PlaceWare eMeeting
technology, Kern's employees focus on how to make sure their
call builds the relationship.

Kern says, "The key is to make the eMeeting entertaining
and interactive. We keep the customer involved and the meeting moving forward. Everyone has a short attention span."
Kern Direct Marketing people show great attention and respect
for the customer's time, interacting with them quickly and powerfully. He continues, "Using Web conferencing, I show that I
care about making it convenient and fast for our customers.
That is one way I demonstrate building a relationship."

End the eMeeting with a Tangible Takeaway

If an eTeam is focused on producing a tangible takeaway from their meeting, human nature then engages them to get the job done. By creating live documents during the eMeeting, the team forces itself to get specific. Verbal words alone are too vague. Supplement spoken key points with written ones captured on an online shared whiteboard. Written words on screen make sure the group is in harmony about the essence of the problem, the solutions, the action items, the to-do list, or other critical eMeeting points. The result is communication that is specific, concrete, and tangible for all. When the eMeeting ends, everyone on the eTeam has the same understanding, and each gets a copy of the electronic file as well.

> *Everyone leaves the meeting with a tangible result they created together.*

    Yesterday's way to meet was to create action items and to-do lists to be done outside the meeting. Today's way to meet is to get the action done in our meeting together, live. Any action items or to-do lists are created by and shared by all in a live display on each person's computer. When the meeting ends, the documents are transferred. Everyone leaves the meeting with a tangible result they created together. All those meetings that we have attended where we didn't accomplish anything quickly now become a thing of the past. When you used to go to meet in the small room down the hall, you left with a result. Now virtual meetings are as spontaneous and interactive, and eTeams leave with a result. That's Bionic eTeamwork.

B I O N I C

eTeamwork Checklist

How to Build Bionic eMeetings

This chapter began with a quote. "People vote with their mouse. They will log on to a meeting if it is meaningful or worthwhile. They will log off if it is not."

If your eTeam's meetings fail to engage, you clearly are wasting the team's most valuable resource: their time to connect and interact at HyperSpeed.

To be successful, Bionic eLeaders know that today's eMeetings require more than a well planned agenda. They require mastery of new best practices and new technology to make the eMeeting fast, engaging, and results driven.

Bionic eLeaders conduct engaging eMeetings at the speed of light, using these key best practices.

☐ Don't eMeet to share information; eMeet to collaborate, build teamwork, and get results.

☐ Create a meeting ROI that creates real teamwork.

☐ Use new methods to accelerate human interaction in team meetings.

☐ Input eWarmth.

☐ End the meeting with a tangible takeaway.

THINGS YOU CAN DO TODAY TO
Create Bionic eMeetings

eLeaders	eTeams	Individuals
Become highly skilled in the best practices for leading fast, collaborative eMeetings.	Become highly skilled in the best practices for creating fast, interactive, collaborative eMeetings.	Become highly skilled in the best practices for creating fast, interactive, collaborative eMeetings.
• Decide which technologies help you create fast, cohesive eMeetings. • Get training that helps you master the new technology and best practices. • Create a specific plan to improve eMeetings for your team. • Create norms for using technology's power to drive faster, more cohesive eMeetings.	• All eTeam members must be as skilled as the eLeader, as new eMeeting best practices require everyone to understand how to leverage their power to connect the team. • Create norms that enhance team collaboration in eMeetings.	• Web conference technology lets you create a significantly warmer communication environment. • Decide ways you can use that technology to create more interaction, more trust, and more collaboration, from afar.

The Bionics of Effective 24/7 eCollaboration

10

Question: Does your team have a team Web site?
Answer: Yes, of course.
Question: How often do you use it?
Answer: Never.

Mary called from one of the world's most well-known charities. She handles all press releases in her region, their online and paper newsletters, and all documents that relate to the charity's image in the communities she serves. Every document requires her to refine and complete it with people who don't work where she does.

She said, "It is so difficult to do all of this with e-mail. I have to send out the draft of the newsletter to five people. Usually, it goes out as an attachment to an e-mail message. Each of the five makes changes to it. And then they send it back to me."

To make matters more complex, the newsletter is an iterative process. It will make the rounds to the team no fewer than three separate times before they commit it to print or upload it to the Web site.

Mary said, "This would be a whole lot easier if we worked in one place. Technology just seems to get in the way."

In reality, technology wasn't the problem. The team was using the wrong technology for the job. The technology they used got in the way of collaboration. Their methods were slow and ineffective. Nothing about their process created a team environment.

Bionic eTeams have a whole different experience in collaborating in a 24/7 environment.

The expression 24/7 means 24 hours a day, 7 days a week. Teams might need to collaborate in a 24/7 environment if their work spans multiple time zones; e.g., a team whose members must collaborate together from South America, Asia, and Europe. The local normal workday schedules of such a widely dispersed team never overlap.

> *People don't have to collaborate in real time to work as a team.*

Teams don't have to cover the globe to want better ways to collaborate 24/7. Teams can be in the same time zone and want it. Teams whose work revolves around creating, editing, and managing multiple versions of documents of any type may want to collaborate 24/7. Marketing campaigns, publicity campaigns, product documentation, product design and development, convention planning, service troubleshooting—these are only a few examples of collaboration that can be done effectively 24/7. People that are in the same time zone, but in different locations, may improve collaboration and speed results with 24/7 approach.

People don't have to collaborate in real time to work as a team. This chapter features some exemplary Bionic eTeams that light the way to successful 24/7 collaboration. Some have taken the small-group approach, with prepackaged or Internet-based 24/7 technologies that anyone can buy, license, and use. The Chute Gerdeman example you saw in Chapter 5 took the small group approach.

Others have taken the corporatewide approach, spending millions to create a customized online community to facilitate human communication. The Merrill Lynch example you saw in Chapter 6 and the Xerox example you'll meet in this chapter took the corporatewide approach.

Plunking some 24/7 technology into your team's arsenal will not ensure that people will collaborate in a noninteractive environment. That approach will almost certainly ensure failure. In fact, that is why many teams that tried 24/7 technology found it ineffective or stopped using it. Read this chapter, and try it again.

The teams you are about to meet were successful because they approached their 24/7 technology as a key part of their team's eCommunity. Their success wasn't because of the technology. It was because of the way humans used that technology to create Bionic eTeamwork. The human side is always the first concern.

Small eTeam 24/7 Collaboration

Small teams have wonderful options for 24/7 collaboration on documents. Which one is best for you depends on the level of version control that you need. You can choose from many more tools than this book has the space to cover. The two that you will read about next stand at the front of the line. Used effectively, they launch a team into HyperSpeed.

Let's look at how two Bionic eTeams found success using different 24/7 approaches to online collaboration.

Prepackaged Group Collaboration Software

Take Ann Balaban, a member of the ASIC Documentation Team at Texas Instruments. The team of ten in Texas and four in India created highly technical data books, user manuals, and product sheets. Consumer electronics manufacturers and telecommunications companies like Nokia and Motorola need this documentation to integrate application-specific integrated circuits into their own systems. The documentation must be accurate, complete, and on time.

When Texas Instruments was doing only one release at a time, this eTeam's challenge was huge. Then speed kicked in. Integrated circuit releases increased to two, then three, then four at a time. Balaban said, "We were absolutely over-whelmed! We worked 14 to 16 hours a day. We were up at 3 AM getting a release out. We realized that we just couldn't continue to work like this."

So their eTeam became proactive about how to use tech-nology to support teamwork. "We got together and auto-mated. Then we flew," Balaban said. And fly they did! They reduced a process that used to take two to three weeks to two to three days. In one year, they published almost 800 percent more pages. They saved $1 million in costs each year for doc-umentation. Best of all, Balaban states, "Our information is up-to-date and more accurate . . . ."

How did they do it? They created, edited, exchanged, and published their documentation via the Web using Adobe Acro-bat Exchange and Adobe Framemaker. They streamlined their document authoring and review process as a team, con-necting better with their customers and each other.

Adobe Acrobat Exchange lets people in Texas and India collaborate on wording, edits, content, and illustrations. Any-one could annotate the document with an electronic version of sticky-notes, markers, and keyboard changes. They could attach files, references, and even verbal notices. Then, with a simple click and drag, the document owner could pool every-one's edits into a single summary document. The document owner could refer to the summary document when making final changes on the original document.

Balaban said, "We are way above the norm on speed. We get a lot more done than any other document team. When we go to conferences, it is difficult to get input because no one is where we are." That's Bionic eTeamwork!

The important point to note here is that putting Acrobat on everyone's desktop did not create this success. Instead, this team examined its documentation process from the customer to the chip designers to the documentation experts. They revamped the entire process, creating a clear and specific plan as to how they would use Acrobat to make their work faster and more effective. Now they're at HyperSpeed.

Online Electronic Teamroom

If versions change, grow, and evolve rapidly, you'll want to choose an internet-based (or commercial) version of an electronic teamroom. Balaban's Bionic eTeam used this technology to track version changes and collaborate at lightspeed.

Wendy Johnson, a leader at Chute Gerdeman, the retail design firm that you met in Chapter 5, talked about how her team used it to improve communication with clients. Chute Gerdeman was developing a new brand and packaging for a pharmaceutical company in a different state.

> *eRoom was not used in isolation. The team often combined it with conference calls, e-mail, and onsite visits.*

The team made a trip to the client site to do onsite interviews and rapport building. They used that time to interact with the client and create a common language about the client's preferences. Within days after returning to the office, they placed ideas in their war eRoom for the client to see. Later, they conferenced with the client by phone, as each pulled up the file from eRoom.

Importantly, eRoom was not used in isolation. The team often combined it with conference calls, e-mail, and onsite visits. It gave everyone on the team a single place to connect with critical team information and to then collaborate with it. Johnson remarked, "It helped us build real teamwork."

> *"Some people think that dropping a technology into a team environment will instantly create teamwork. It doesn't."*

Maridan A. Clements of Philips Components eBusiness gives electronic teamroom technology high marks, as well. She has been instrumental in helping teams at Philips use technology to support high performance teamwork. "An electronic team-room is an essential tool for project managers," she said.

She continued, "Some people think that dropping a technology into a team environment will instantly create teamwork. It doesn't." No matter what technology virtual teams use, teamwork is a human process. People need to feel that they belong and are a part of the team. Then the technology must support and grow that team's ability to collaborate.

Clements graciously shares five best practices that she has learned during her extensive use of electronic teamrooms. These best practices focus on how to build sense of team when using this tool:

1. *Be consistent.* Have a clear plan for how to use your electronic teamroom as a team. For example, set the norm to post all documents in the eTeamRoom, not attach any to e-mails. Sometimes, some gentle reminders may be needed to adjust communication to this norm. Stay with it.

2. *Involve everyone.* Give everyone the rights to see and participate. Exclude no one.

3. *Set times to look at documents together.* Get on the phone, have everyone pull up the document, and discuss it. When the team is coming up on a deliverable, use Web conference technology and electronic teamroom technology together.

4. *Stay very organized and structured so people don't get frustrated.* If people can't find something, they will give up quickly. Some will want to stop using the teamroom altogether. Put a table of contents up front to make it easy for people to find what they want.

5. *Use graphics and photos.* We use these everywhere. It adds a more human touch. Right now we are having a logo contest. Once the team selects a winner, we're going to have T-shirts printed for everyone on the team to wear.

In summary, Bionic-level collaboration doesn't happen on the fly. Teams must determine what specific collaboration they need to do at Bionic levels. They need to identify the right tool, create a specific plan on how that tool will be used for eTeam collaboration, and then make sure everyone is trained to use it at the highest level. Some teams employ a project manager just to get organized. Once you lay that powerful foundation, the payoffs in eTeam speed and cohesion are immense.

Thanks to an array of powerful, yet easy-to-use 24/7 collaborative technologies, Bionic eTeams can work together at high levels anywhere, all the time. As you've seen, people don't have to be in the same place or time zone to work together in very human ways.

Large Group 24/7 Collaboration

What do leaders need to know about getting hundreds or thousands of people to collaborate 24/7 all over the globe?

Corporate leaders have made a Herculean effort to build a technology infrastructure for global success. They no longer invest just to own the latest technology on the block. Instead, technology enables people who span many time zones to collaborate, connect, and perform. Leaders have spent billions on upgrading networks, software, hardware, intranets, and extranets. They've spent billions more designing elegant capability into their Web technology.

Teams must identify the right tool, create a specific plan on how that tool will be used for eTeam collaboration, and then make sure everyone is trained to use it at the highest level.

Web sites are more packed with information. Web sites are exciting to look at, amazing to interact with, and extraordinarily fast in giving us the information we want. With a click of a mouse, people can search by keywords, play videos, hear audio, contribute to a chat, and join Web conferences from anywhere in the world. At last, the Web breaks down the barrier of "place." With the click of a mouse, anyone anywhere in the world can access the same information or each other.

Yet, despite the fanciest Web technology, eTeams still have major problems. Critical knowledge, best practices, and resources remain isolated in pockets. Learning isn't leveraged across sites. After a decade of blockbuster investments, the people on the worldwide sales and service team fail to leverage their talent and processes worldwide through their Web site. The company's engineers in London aren't collaborating across time zones with the engineers in Germany, India, and Africa. The people in Asia are upset about having less access to corporate resources, like training and a real-time response, than the people in North America. Everyone learns separately, instead of together. In short, eTeams *can* connect through their Web technology. In reality, though, they are still divided by time and space.

> At last, the Web breaks down the barrier of "place."

Don't blame technology. Today's elegant technology is so well designed and so intuitive that few of us even need to use the online help guide. With rare exceptions, we jump right in and start clicking. Instead, the problem is how eTeams use Web sites to connect on a human and a performance level.

To compete in the global marketplace, people serve customers in locations all over the globe. A customer in Hong Kong expects more than the finest technical support of the Pacific Rim. He expects the best available support anywhere in the *world*—as of that moment in time. So do customers in Europe, North America, South America, the Middle East, and every other place on the planet. People want problems fixed now, handled now, corrected now, responded to now, and completed now. The people in Singapore don't want to wait overnight for a response during the next business day in New York. Overnight is too slow—too unresponsive for today's fast marketplace. In the Third Millennium, a team's response to its customers must be now—immediately.

If you want your people to interact and build team independent of time or place, then don't build a Web site. Add psychology to how the eTeam will use the technology. Become Bionic: build a Web site eCommunity.

The 24/7 Bionic eCommunity

Successful eTeam Web sites don't just share information. They are designed to attract and build an eCommunity. Community is a critical word. Accessing the same Web site does not make people into a community. Instead, community is about forging and reinforcing human connections.

> *Overnight is too slow—too unresponsive for today's fast marketplace.*

It is a place where people create something better together than they can create alone, as individuals. A community is where people come together to share, interact, and support each other. It is a place full of life—covering the full spectrum of life's experiences, from failure to success and opportunity to reward. In a community, people reach out to lend a helping hand, pulling each other up. It feels good to be in a community because we belong.

Most importantly, community is a place where no one feels alone.

The problem is that in most eTeam Web sites, people *feel* alone because they *are* alone. The Web site is not designed to create community. The key to success, then, is not for Bionic eLeaders to build a Web site, but to build a Web site eCommunity. That's what Bionic eLeader Howard Sorgen built at Merrill Lynch with the Trusted Global Advisor initiative. That's what Bionic eLeader Tom Ruddy, Global Eureka Manager at Xerox did, too.

> *Community is about forging and reinforcing human connections. It is a place full of life— covering the full spectrum of life's experiences, from failure to success and opportunity to reward.*

You may have heard Xerox's advertisements to "keep the conversation going." How do you keep a constant 24/7 conversation going among 24,000 service engineers on every continent around the world? Dr. Tom Ruddy knows, because he led the development of more than a successful Web site for Xerox repair technicians. He led the development of an extraordinarily powerful 24/7 Web site eCommunity that circles the world. *Eureka!* is its name. Xerox's customer service engineers worldwide connect through Eureka! to share problems, solutions, and best practices.

> *The problem is that in most eTeam Web sites, people feel alone because they are alone.*

One key foundation for Eureka!'s success was focusing first on the eCommunity. Ruddy said, "If you spend more than 30 percent on the technical side, you will fail. Spend 70 percent of your time on the behavioral side—the people side of this." Smart move!

Some people think of community as a place. In reality, it isn't. Instead, community is an environment we create for ourselves. We may experience community while in a physical place. But place is not where the community resides. Community is with the people—all pulling together to create something better together than they can create alone. Community is not about taking, accessing, or finding. It is about giving, interacting, and joining together. An eCommunity is not bound by place, but instead is bound by a common theme: to pool our resources as a group to create success together.

If you want success, start first with the people side. Then add the technology side.

Four Critical Parts of a 24/7 eCommunity

Effective Web site eCommunities have a common structure that is designed to make high-quality interaction happen. If you want to create an eCommunity or transform your Web site into one, start with a foundation of these four components.

None of these four components is one-dimensional. Each is multidimensional, like a multilevel checkers game you can play on your computer. One doesn't deal with just one level but many in an effective Web site eCommunity.

Multilevel ROI: Return on Interaction

When you invest in stocks, you want a high return on your investment. When you visit a Web site eCommunity, you want an even higher return. After all, you can always earn more money, but none of us can buy any more time. As the pace of business goes faster, people require higher value out of how they use their time.

Every visit to the eCommunity must deliver tangible value, quickly—on multiple levels. Take this story from Xerox's Eureka! Web site eCommunity. With a steady stream of new copiers, new updates, and new capabilities coming out every day, staying current on how to fix a wide variety of rapidly advancing machines is no easy task. Keeping a whole service force of technicians around the world current on how to fix these machines seems even more daunting. Without an effective Web site eCommunity, each service technician stands alone. With the Eureka! Web site eCommunity, however, the technicians pool together.

> *As the pace of business goes faster, people require higher value out of how they use their time.*

Take one customer in São Paulo, Brazil, who had purchased a new DocuColor, a digital color copier that costs about $40,000. Because of a series of intermittent problems that just wouldn't go away, Xerox was about to replace the whole machine to keep the customer happy. Luckily, one of the technicians there had just received training in Eureka! He went to Eureka! to find a solution. A technician in Canada had encountered the problem and suggested a 50¢ solution that solved it. The machine worked. The problem didn't come back. That 50¢ solution gained a happy customer. And it saved $40,000 for Xerox.

Look at the multilevel Return on Interaction that happened because of Eureka!

- Eureka! created a high ROI for the customer. The problem was fixed. The machine worked like a charm. The customer was happy.

- Eureka! created a high ROI for the technician in Brazil. Eureka! gave the technician a new way to fix the problem fast and effectively. It helped the technician create a happy customer experience with Xerox.

- Eureka! created a high ROI for the technician in Canada. Eureka let him share a best practice that helped someone else and the company. The technician in Canada received a positive response from the technician in São Paulo who used the solution.

- Eureka! created a high ROI for Xerox. The expense to correct the problem and keep the customer happy was 50¢, not $40,000.

What kind of conversations do you think stories like this generate to build excitement about the eCommunity? Eureka! was a grass roots program that became a significant success story at Xerox. It grew rapidly because, first of all, it delivered a high ROI on so many levels.

With Ruddy's leadership, Xerox's Eureka! eCommunity was already traveling at the speed of light around world—and it's getting even better. They accelerate Eureka's ROI with visual cues—attaching diagrams, documents, and photographs. They're adding audio cues—attaching sound wave files. The file might say, "If you hear this clicking sound, replace this part now. If you don't, in 1,000 copies the part will go bad." And they accelerate Eureka's draw with touch (through the keyboard) cues that reinforce the eCommunity: the multilevel "RFI" that you'll read about in a minute.

Frequently the odor of the machine indicates problems, as well. Ruddy said, "When we learn how to add a sense of smell, the technicians will have everything they need." Interesting thought!

Multilevel RFI: Reward/Recognition for Interaction

If you want people to do something new, reward and recognize them. Make the reward and recognition fast, tangible, and specific. To create an effective eCommunity, however, don't stop there. You'll need to generate a significantly higher amount of metaphorical eMileage (or eKilometers) when people visit and contribute to the eCommunity. You'll need to create a multilevel RFI: Reward and Recognition for Interaction.

The most significant reward is that the visit to the eCommunity produces a tangible return on a personal level. Basically, it helps you do your job better. It helps you make your customer happier, your life easier, your result better, your brain smarter, and your personal resources broader and more valuable. Yes, money works too.

> *The eCommunity helps you make your customer happier, your life easier, your result better, your brain smarter, and your personal resources broader and more valuable. Yes, money works too.*

But that's not enough. To build eCommunity, multilevel reward and recognition must occur each time the eCommunity is used. Ruddy was masterful in building in multiple levels of reward and recognition every time a technician use Eureka! Each level enhanced the eCommunity. Let's look at a few:

- When a technician offered a solution, her name appeared at the top of the written best practice list on Eureka! The name gave the technician visibility with her peers.

- When a technician used a solution, he posted a thumbs up or thumbs down—indicating that the solution did or didn't work.

- When a technician used a solution, the eCommunity system made it easy for the technician to extend an "ePat on the back" note to the person who offered the solution.

- The eCommunity system automatically tallied how many solutions worked, who offered the most solutions, and which sites offered the most solutions. That information was used to bestow lavish rewards and recognition to reinforce the eCommunity.

- The Eureka! eCommunity had a Hall of Fame for the technicians who offered the most useful tips. The award quantified how many tips the technician created and how many hours were saved around the world because of that tip. This recognition showed everyone what was important, and the recognition was more than Hall of Fame status. Recognition also included cash and other rewards.

Ruddy's whole approach ensured that useful, workable solutions were online, thereby increasing the value of the Web site to the members of the Eureka! eCommunity. Importantly, rewards and recognition didn't happen at one level. They were used on multiple levels to reinforce the strength, power, and effectiveness of the eCommunity.

Dynamic at Multiple Levels

If a Web site isn't dynamic, changing, and up to date—people stop going.

> Dynamic isn't about creating an information dump. Instead, dynamic means that the Web site is designed for interaction, change, and creating value on many levels.

Dynamic isn't about creating an information dump. Anyone can design a Web site and dump "stuff." Instead, dynamic means that the Web site is designed for interaction, change, and creating value on many levels. Dynamic is also about the way people interact while at the eCommunity. The dynamics aren't put in the Web site just for fun. Dynamics are carefully designed to build and reinforce the quality of the eCommunity.

No one person or site can create an effective eCommunity. Instead, its success must be built on the contributions of everyone who belongs to it. In fact, this concept is so critical for success, that we have given it a name: eSURFdom. If you want to SURF the eCommunity, you have to contribute your fair share. Hence, eSURFdom.

The term eSURFdom is not about slavery or bondage. It definitely is not a name I created to be cute. Instead, it is a *metaphor about an expected contribution*—a portion that everyone has to give in order for the community to build its success. Without taxes, our physical communities couldn't build roads, schools, power systems, or defense. Without eSURFdom, our eCommunity can't build the quality knowledge infrastructure and interaction it needs for success. Whether it is a click, a comment, or a detailed solution—everyone adds to the validity, value, and quality of our eCommunity resources.

> *Without eSURFdom, our eCommunity can't build the quality knowledge infrastructure and interaction it needs for success.*

Therefore, the keys to creating a dynamic eCommunity are built from a careful plan that starts with people, then adds technology.

- How to bring a steady stream of quality problems, solutions, and knowledge to the eCommunity.

- How to reinforce and build on that knowledge by eCommunity participants.

- How to eliminate and control monstrous volumes of "stuff" that want to invade your eCommunity.

About 7 percent of Eureka!'s eCommunity members spend one to three hours a week screening solutions that are offered by other Xerox technicians all over the world. If a solution is repeatable, that tip is shared on Eureka! About 1,000 pieces of information every month are published for the eCommunity on Eureka!

If every technician had to read all 1,000 pieces, they wouldn't have any time to go fix the machines. Yet, every technician needs quality solutions to do his job better.

Eureka! controls the overload by subscriptions based on product. The technicians for the Docutek machines will receive only those new tips that were created and validated for that specific product. Instead of trying to stay on top of 1,000 updates a month, an average technician around the world might only need to read 30 updates. That's about one a day. When a new best practice is placed on the Web site, the technician gets a prompt to check it out. Learning is constant, relevant, and of high value.

Behind the scenes of Eureka!'s success is a global network of people who constantly work the site, leverage the feedback, bring forth problems, and resolve issues to make it work.

Human eUpgrading

Trends for the Third Millennium are clear. Elegant technology will evolve at an ever faster pace. Teams can no longer afford to use 10 percent of technology's power. They just won't be fast enough.

To compete, teams must integrate technology in ways that dramatically increase collaboration and productivity. Bionic eTeams know that software gets upgraded all the time. Bionic eTeams make it a point also to upgrade human ability to collaborate with it. Whether eUpgrading is done with an onsite class or a virtual one, it is about improving human skills and best practices on technology—hence the *e.*

> *Bionic eTeams know that software gets upgraded all the time. Bionic eTeams make it a point also to upgrade human ability to collaborate with it.*

When Xerox rolled out Eureka!, their service technicians worldwide were trained in how to use it. The training helped them understand that Eureka! was a dynamic two-way process that was constantly going on. Everyone had to learn how to communicate and talk through their eCommunity.

The Trusted Global Advisor eCommunity that Merrill Lynch created for its financial consultants was supported with training as well. The Trusted Global Advisor was such a technical leap forward, new workstations were rolled out site by site. Howard Sorgen wanted people to understand and fully use its resources. In the initial rollout, Merrill Lynch sent teams of people to provide human eUpgrading to this system. Some were onsite, others were human help desks, and still others provided eMentoring support. By the end of this training, people knew how to navigate the system and use its power to deliver higher levels of service to customers.

Once people had mastery of the Trusted Global Advisor platform, Merrill Lynch continued to provide human eUpgrading. Each workstation could link to three channels for learning. One interacted with the business analysts who upgraded the consultant's knowledge of current products. Another channel was CNBC, which upgraded the consultant on market news. And the third was their Learning Channel. Any time new functionality was added to their eCommunity workstation, the financial consultants could get training on how to use it.

Most importantly, Sorgen's and Ruddy's systems built in feedback mechanisms whereby they, as the Governors, so to speak, of their respective eCommunities, could get feedback about their use. When Sorgen rolled out new functionality to the members of the Trusted Global Advisor eCommunity, their Learning Channel provided just-in-time programs to train people to use that resource or function of their system. Five days later, Sorgen was able to assess how many people used the new functionality or resource. In a similar way, Ruddy's system provided feedback on how many of their service engineers accessed the system, which best practices were accessed most, which saved the most human hours of work, and other data. This feedback was used to continue to refine and build the power of the systems to create Bionic eTeamwork.

B I O N I C

eTeamwork Checklist

How to Build Bionic 24/7 eCollaboration

This chapter began with the quote:

Question: Does your team have a team Web site?
Answer: Yes, of course.
Question: How often do you use it?
Answer: Never.

If your eTeam's Web site, electronic teamroom, or other 24/7 collaborative technology has failed to make a difference in your team, the problem isn't the technology. It is how the people are using it.

For small teams, stop trying to collaborate by e-mail with attachments. Those methods are in the Dark Ages. Get up to speed with Adobe Acrobat Exchange. Possibly add electronic teamroom capability if it will make document exchange faster. Assign a project manager to organize your electronic teamroom so everyone can access and edit documents quickly. Only put key documents in the electronic teamroom and make sure they are easy to find, or people will quickly lose interest.

For larger teams, don't build a Web site. Build an eCommunity. An eCommunity is a dynamic, interactive place where people connect on a human and performance level. Putting up a Web site and dumping material on it is not the answer. Start first with your people, specifically the eCommunity you want to create and support. Then add technology to build, reinforce, and sustain that community.

Bionic eLeaders create a 24/7 eCommunity by:

☐ Multilevel ROI—Return on Interaction

☐ Multilevel RFI—Reward/Recognition for Interaction

☐ Dynamics at Multiple Levels

☐ Human eUpgrading

THINGS YOU CAN DO TODAY TO
Create Bionic 24/7 eCollaboration

eLeaders	eTeams	Individuals
Help your team define the eCommunity it wants to create 24/7. • Then add the ways the Web site (or electronic teamroom) creates its ROI, RFI, and Dynamic quality. • Make sure everyone participates in creating the site, and then is trained in how to use it at high levels. • Ensure the site is kept up to date. If it becomes a graveyard, people may not even visit it on Memorial Day! • If you cannot commit to all of these things, don't do an eTeam Web site.	Determine what 24/7 collaboration would enhance teamwork and interaction on the team. • Determine the right technology: Acrobat Exchange and/or electronic teamroom capability. • Have a project manager organize it and keep after it. • Make sure people follow the rules for the 24/7 collaboration environment that the team creates. • Assess how well the site improves collaboration, and make adjustments as needed.	You may not need to use a Web site for 24/7 collaboration. • If you do have a need to collaborate 24/7, identify the collaborative software you want to use (e.g., Adobe Acrobat). • Then get training in how to use it at Bionic levels. • Contribute to the eCommunity. Be a vital part of it.

11

Bionic
eTeamwork

A Choice and a Commitment

> *It's your technology. How we develop it and how it evolves will depend as much on you [the consumer] as it will on any of the [software and Internet CEOs on the Silicon Summit II panel].*
> **Tom Brokaw**

The definition of insanity is doing the same thing over and over again, expecting a different result. Why do we get trapped into staying where we don't want to be? Becoming Bionic is a choice and a commitment—with big payoffs!

No matter how much technology teams have around them, the ones that excel attend first to the human side of eTeamwork. Then they add technology to speed the process and enhance the human connections.

Here are the key ways you can create fast, cohesive Bionic eTeamwork.

> *No matter how much technology teams have around them, the ones that excel attend first to the human side of eTeamwork.*

Prepare People for HyperSpeed

HyperSpeed isn't about technology. It's about how people use technology to create fast, cohesive eTeamwork. Bionic eTeams use technology to collaborate, solve problems, build sense of team, create buy-in, build trust, and create results— exponentially faster and more effectively than ever before.

Technology is intuitive. How people use it to connect isn't. So Bionic eTeams take great care to become Power Users, focusing mostly on how to use technology to collaborate together with great speed and humanity.

> *Today's teams are virtual—dispersed around the world, in dire need of a human connection.*

If you want faster decisions, faster teamwork, faster rapport, faster buy-in, faster collaboration—faster anything related to human teamwork or perfor- mance—you won't get it if you stay in methods that are designed for a differ- ent era. Very few teams work in one lo- cation. Today's teams are virtual— dispersed around the world, in dire need of a human connec- tion that matches what we used to create when team members worked in one place.

Bionic eTeamwork is not about technology. It is about human eTeamwork that is supported and enhanced by the way people collaborate through technology.

Create InTouch

> *High-trust relation- ships are manda- tory for inspired eTeamwork.*

InTouch is more than high-tech, high- touch communication. InTouch is about going to the next level: creating a hu- man bond, a human connection, and/or sense of team with people that span the globe. InTouch will happen if people want it to happen and jointly take action to create it.

High-trust relationships are mandatory for inspired eTeam- work. As such, Bionic eLeaders and eTeams follow a consistent plan to build InTouch both during onsite meetings as well as when communicating virtually.

Create and Amplify Human Moments of Truth

eTeams function in a feedback vacuum. Today's managers aren't down the hall; they're thousands of miles away. They have so many direct reports across so many different locations, that one-to-one spontaneous feedback has nearly disappeared. The result is a huge disconnect that no charter, vision, value statement, or goal statement can fill. The disconnect is a human disconnect: the leader, the team, the customer, and the work.

> *Moments of Truth give eTeams a specific, concrete lightpost to guide their work, their collaboration, and their sense of team.*

Like a magnifying glass, Moments of Truth focus people on the human side of success—the behaviors that make customers happy and lead directly to success. Moments of Truth give eTeams a specific, concrete lightpost to guide their work, their collaboration, and their sense of team. In today's eTeams, no leader can wander around enough to create this kind of focus, positive mindset, and motivation.

Build Sense of Team, from Afar

Today's virtual team suffers from too much information and not enough communication. The better people feel, the better work they will do, and the happier they will be. Bionic eLeaders diligently build sense of team by communicating about the human experience of creating and winning success.

Legends are built of stories, struggles, and triumphs. eLeaders create eMotion about these three sense of team themes:

1. *eMotion around the human stories of past and present progress.* From separate locations, people can only see their own progress. Bionic eLeaders and eTeams amplify past and present success, highlighting the

human experience behind the metrics, the tag lines, and the eTeam buzz.

2. *eMotion around preparing for future motion or success.* Here the Bionic eLeader becomes the teacher and coach, helping people understand the background behind key initiatives, responses to changing customer needs, and other keys to success.

3. *eMotion about the team itself.* This communication has a singular focus: make people feel good about the team's important work, the way it serves its customers, and the way people work together. Focus every story on the very personal and very human side of the team and the team's work.

Create Engaging eMeetings

> *Bionic eLeaders make eMeetings warm, putting a human face on the visuals, words, and interaction.*

The world is moving too fast for people to waste time in boring, slow, unproductive eMeetings. Bionic eLeaders are proactive in using new methods and new technologies that enable faster, more interactive, more spontaneous eMeetings. Bionic eTeams only meet about ROI topics, topics that give a high return on interactive time. They plan the eMeeting for speedy human interaction, using ePolling and other Web conference features to make decisions faster, collaborate faster, build buy-in faster, and build teamwork faster. Lastly, Bionic eLeaders make eMeetings warm, putting a human face on the visuals, words, and interaction. Everyone leaves the meeting with a printed copy of the eMeeting deliverable.

Create Bionic 24/7 eCollaboration

Stop trying to collaborate by e-mail with attachments. Small teams create Bionic eTeamwork through the way they use

Adobe Acrobat Exchange, electronic teamroom technology, or other 24/7 collaborative tools. Create a specific plan for how to use technology in ways that build team. If needed, have a project manager set it up and organize it. Simplicity is key.

Larger organizations build Bionic eTeamwork through a custom-built, Web-based, 24/7 eCommunity. A community is not a place where people browse or take information. It is a place where everyone contributes to an evolving, changing, high-value, quality eCommunity. An effective eCommunity creates a high-value ROI, creating a high return that impacts many levels of the community. It provides a multilevel

> *The eCommunity builds in dynamic interaction at many levels, with every point, click, or comment creating value for all.*

RFI, a reward and recognition program, for interaction in the eCommunity Web site. The eCommunity builds in dynamic interaction at many levels, with every point, click, or comment creating value for all. And most importantly, the eCommunity is supported with training. Training raises the technical acumen on that Web site to its highest level. As the Web site adds functionality, training is added, as well.

Create the Courage to Commit

Now you know what you need to do to be successful building a faster, more cohesive team—a Bionic eTeam. You also know the winning formula for Bionic eTeamwork: start first with the human side of eTeamwork, then add technology. The result is a team that communicates effectively when people are together, with no compromise when people are apart. What you'll discover is this: people don't have to work in one place to be a real team—interactive, high-trust, and energized.

One very wise man I have known in my life—my Dad— once said, "Success isn't going to come knocking on your door. You have to choose it. Then you have to commit yourself to creating it." His words have stayed with me for a lifetime, acting like a guiding star that I still look to daily. Now let me modify his wise message for you.

Bionic eTeamwork isn't going to come knocking on your door. It is not a natural evolution that will happen on its own. You won't evolve to that level unless you choose it and commit to it. Without that choice and commitment, you will be trapped in the Disabled and Mechanical stages. You'll feel frustrated about virtual teamwork, and so will your virtual team.

> *Bionic eTeamwork isn't going to come knocking on your door. It is not a natural evolution that will happen on its own. You won't evolve to that level unless you choose it and commit to it.*

When Chuck Yeager broke the sound barrier, he changed the course of aviation history. Until his historic flight on the Bell X-1 research plane (now on display at the Smithsonian Museum in Washington, D.C.), no one knew if he would be successful as he pushed the envelope to 700 miles per hour. The closer he got to Mach 1—the speed of sound—the more the plane rattled, shook, and did a host of other frightening things. Despite the challenge, Yeager wouldn't break his commitment to go the distance, literally. Breaking the sound barrier was his number one priority. No way was he going to back down or miss an opportunity to change the world.

Yeager had the technology. He had his good brain and his lifetime of experience. He had the opportunity. He knew he could do it, and he was determined not to let anything stand in his way. He was a barrier buster, and he was successful. Although his classified flight happened on October 14, 1947, it was not announced to the public until 1948—except for the supersonic boom, of course! Amazingly, after he broke through the sound barrier, the plane stopped rattling and soared smoothly. The fast, yet smooth ride is what your team will feel when you become Bionic.

Bionic eLeaders tap into that same kind of determination in creating Bionic eTeamwork. Before any team can evolve to Bionic, it has to want to become Bionic: fast and cohesive, with little to no face time. It has to want to break the place barrier—with no compromise in the excitement and joy that working virtually can have. The eLeader must recognize that groups can get things done by e-mail and conference calls, but can get extraordinary things done by attending to the human side of eTeamwork. Happy, satisfied, motivated people will easily outproduce people who are just getting by and sending e-mail messages to each other.

Bionic eTeamwork Is within Your Reach!

In summary, Bionic eTeamwork is about an inspired, very human level of teamwork. Although Bionic has a technology component, the value of the technology comes only from how people use it to create trust, collaboration, and sense of team. Teams do not evolve to Bionic naturally. *Bionic eTeamwork is created only when eLeaders and eTeams choose it, commit to it, and do the work necessary to achieve it.* The result is a team that has built the human bridges it needs to be exceptionally fast and cohesive in a far-flung, high-technology, global workplace.

> *Happy, satisfied, motivated people will easily outproduce people who are just getting by and sending e-mail messages to each other.*

Steve Austin seeks a career change, but isn't sure what opportunities await him. As he browses Monster.com, he sees a job posting for a Bionic eTeam Leader. He fires off his résumé, happy to have found an opportunity that uses some of his best talents.

Minutes later, he hears the familiar chime that an e-mail has just arrived in Outlook. Amazingly, it is an e-mail with a hotlink to a Web conference site. He clicks, and in seconds he and Ms. Carolyn Peters, the HR Manager, are in a live video conference link from their separate desktops.

"It's a pleasure to meet you, Mr. Austin," Ms. Peters says. "Let me tell you a little bit about our company. We aren't like every other company, Mr. Austin. We have to be better, faster, and stronger than everyone else."

"I understand," says Austin. "The job posting on your Web site said you are looking for a Bionic eLeader. As you can see from my résumé, I am the Bionic Man. I was designed to be better, faster, and stronger. Can you tell me, Ms. Peters, what qualifications are you looking for, specifically?"

Ms. Peters leans forward slightly at her desk and says, "First, we need a leader with speed."

Austin thinks to himself *Bingo! Right on!* Smiling, he says, "Speed is something I'm very very good at. You know that with my bionic legs, I can run at 60 mph! I can jump the length of a football field. They're extraordinarily strong and fast."

Ms. Peters respectfully acknowledges his noteworthy speed, then she adds. "We're running at the speed of light now, Mr. Austin. Not only do you need to be fast, but your eTeam needs to be fast."

Austin gulps, then says, "The speed of light? I knew things were changing fast, but I didn't realize just how fast. Maybe I can get an upgrade."

"We've learned, Mr. Austin, that it's no longer enough just to upgrade technology. To be fast enough for our demanding customers, we always upgrade our human skills on technology, too. No one here is satisfied with using only 10 percent of technology's power. We want our people to know how to leverage all 100 percent of its ability to connect us," Ms. Peters says, pausing for a moment. "Second, we need a leader with an eye for success."

Austin sits a little more forward in his seat, a little closer to the camera, and says, "You know, Ms. Peters, I have a bionic eye! I can read a newspaper four miles away! I can read more than the titles. I can read the small print! Pretty good, isn't it!?"

Ms. Peters smiles again, saying, "Mr. Austin, your vision is far better than mine. For this job posting, however, we are looking for someone who can help the eTeam see what is important and stay focused on what is important. You see, Mr. Austin, this team circles the world. People work from home offices, distant facilities, and other companies around the world. They lose sight about what they've accomplished and what they need to do next. Do you think you can help them see these things better when people aren't face to face? Do you think that you can help them see themselves as a team, see their accomplishments as a team, and see what they need to do to be successful in the future as a team?"

Austin pauses, then says, "I guess a Bionic eye isn't what it used to be. It looks like I'll be upgrading my skills and new best practices to help everyone see their teamwork growing around the world, too."

Ms. Peters likes his attitude and his humanity. "That sounds good, Mr. Austin. Finally, and most important of all, we need someone with a good heart. It's a cold, cruel world out there now that our people don't work in one place. People feel disconnected from each other, their customers, and their work. Tell me about your heart, Mr. Austin. Do you have a Bionic heart that is strong enough for this challenge?"

Austin pauses. He really wants this job, but feels like her third question is going to kill the opportunity. "Ms. Peters, I don't have a Bionic heart. I have a human one. It ticks like everyone else's. It is a warm and generous heart, but it doesn't have any special capabilities, like my legs, arm, and eye. My heart, though, is the single distinguishing factor that makes me a human, not a robot. *My human heart is the critical factor that gives all of my Bionic parts real value.* Without my heart, . . . well, my ability to create magical results that really matter is gone."

"You don't need a Bionic heart, Mr. Austin," interjects Ms. Peters. "In fact, you gave me the exact response I was looking for. A global team only becomes a team when people connect through their humanity, not their e-mail system. Mr. Austin, I am convinced that you are the perfect person to create Bionic eTeamwork. You're hired! Congratulations!"

She continues, "Now, how *fast* can you start . . . ."

INDEX

D r. Jaclyn Kostner is a *leading authority* on the human side of building aligned, motivated, high-trust virtual teams. She is author of *Knights of the Tele-Round Table* (Warner) and *Virtual Leadership: Secrets from the Round Table for the Multi-Site Manager* (Warner), as well as several other books that focus on using technology as a human communication tool.

She has created dozens of onsite and online workshops focused on eLeadership, eTeamwork, and eCollaboration. Always at the cutting edge, she also has created multimedia and other Web-based resources to facilitate fast, interactive collaboration online. Clearly, her passion is helping people discover how technology helps them extend their human reach and human touch.

Her company, Bridge the Distance, delivers consulting, speaking, and workshop services to clients that circle the world, including IBM, Microsoft, Hewlett Packard, Bank of America, Sun Microsystems, Lockheed-Martin, and many other Fortune 100 companies. She has been cited in *The Wall Street Journal, Time, USA Today, Byte Magazine, FastCompany Magazine, CIO Magazine, PM Network,* and many other publications. She has appeared on CNNfn, TBS, CNBC, PBS, and other radio and TV media. She is a frequent keynote speaker at conferences all over the world, including Europe, Saudi Arabia, and North America. She is also a popular online eSeminar presenter, using PlaceWare, WebEx, Centra, Sametime, and WorldCom Net Conference, among many others, to deliver her message to the desktops of people around the world. Her company delivers online and onsite workshops about how to create Bionic eTeamwork.

B ridge the Distance specializes in the art and technology of creating trust and collaboration in virtual groups and organizations.

Bridge the Distance offers a variety of customized, traditional workshops and online eSeminars, titled the *Bionic eTeamwork Performance* Series™, that are focused on transforming virtual teams into Bionic eTeams. Those offerings include:

- Bionic eLeadership
- Bionic eTeamwork
- Bionic eMeetings
- Bionic ePresentations
- Bionic eSales Calls/Events
- Bionic eTeamwork Assessment Tool
- Executive briefings
- Keynote presentations
- Bionic eTeamwork assessment tools
- Consulting services
- Online eCoaching

Check <www.bionicteam.com> for these additional resources:

- Web conference technology resources
- New technologies for dispersed teams, and how eTeams use them to be successful
- Articles and resources
- Upcoming events

For more information, contact:

Jaclyn Kostner, Ph.D., Founder
BRIDGE THE DISTANCE, INC.
8400 East Prentice Avenue, Suite 1500
Englewood, CO 80111
303-791-4499 from anywhere in the world
866-6BIONIC (866-624-6642), toll-free for U.S. calls
info@bionicteam.com

BIONIC eTeamwork

For special discounts on 20 or more copies of *BIONIC eTeamwork: How to Build Collaborative Virtual Teams at HyperSpeed,* please call Dearborn Trade Special Sales at 800-621-9621, extension 4410.

Dearborn™
Trade Publishing
A **Kaplan Professional** Company